## PRAISE FOR "A TIMELY BOOK"

This timely book will open doors for women eager to explore women's rituals within Judaism, but who may be uncertain about where to begin. Here we have a rich amalgam of ceremonies and tools, all practical suggestions for creating rituals, with metaphysical insights into their meaning.

Miriam's Well gently provokes and inspires women to become participants (and not merely observers) in the tested traditions and innovative celebrations Jewish women are today interweaving.

— **SUSAN WEIDMAN SCHNEIDER**
author of JEWISH AND FEMALE;
editor, LILITH, the Jewish women's magazine

Sensitive and informed, **Miriam's Well** will surely sensitize and inform its readers. It affirms the physical along with the spiritual, the biological along with the historical, and manages to emphasize the feminine without depreciating the masculine. Coordinated with the calendar, its reflective quality invites awareness of the special, differentiated quality of moments in time, while its suggestions for appropriate rituals and ceremonies should encourage readers to respond actively to these differences.

Its concreteness gives vitality to its general ideas, and even city-dwellers are likely to begin following the rhythms of the moon under its spell.

— **RABBI EVERETT GENDLER**
Educator, lecturer and author.
Temple Emanuel, Lowell, Mass.

"...recently discovered your book Miriam's Well and am finding it such a joy! We hope to use some of its ritual material in our women's group..."

KAREN ETHELSDATTAR
Editor, Feminist Theological Institute
Newsletter, NYC.

MIRIAM'S WELL
Rituals for Jewish Women Around the Year

PENINA V. ADELMAN

Photos by Ilene Perlman

BIBLIO PRESS ● FRESH MEADOWS, N.Y.

To Perla and Marcus; Bella and Frank,
Jeannette and Sam; Selma and Burt;
and Steve.

Third Printing 1987

Second Printing, December, 1986.

Copyright © 1986 by Penina V. Adelman (Penina Villenchik Adelman)

ISBN 0-939395-00-X Biblio Press, Fresh Meadows, NY 11365-0022.

Library of Congress Catalog No. 84-071828

Adelman, Penina V. (Penina Villenchik)
    Miriam's Well. Rituals for Jewish Women Around the Year.

    Bibliography: p.
        1. Women, Jewish—Religious life.   2. Judaism—
Customs and practices.   I.   Title.
BM726.A27   1986   296.4'43   84-71828
ISBN 0-939395-00-X (pbk.)

First Biblio Press edition; first printing

Art and design by M.J. Design Studio.

Printed in the United States of America.

Cover photo shows dancing and singing with bride-to-be for month of *Elul.* (See Rituals in Progress photos)

Acknowledgments

I am indebted to these women who helped bring this book into being with their support, inspiration, and faith:

Matia Angelou is assistant principal of the Harvard Hillel Children's School in Cambridge, Mass.
Maia Brumberg sings and composes Jewish folk music and teaches reading in Philadelphia.
Sheila Erlbaum teaches voice and interprets for the deaf in Philadelphia.
Lili Goodman (Kokhava), a folklorist, teaches holistic health in Philadelphia.
Lynn Miriam Gottlieb is a rabbi in Albuquerque, New Mexico.
Pam Hoffman (Liba) is a rabbinical student at the Jewish Theological Seminary in New York.
Andrea Cohen-Kiener (Aviva) is principal of the Hebrew High School at Temple Beth Sholom in Manchester, Ct.
Elana Klugman is a social worker and writer in Boston who has contributed to the new edition of *Our Bodies, Ourselves*.
Cynthia Kravetz is a rabbi in Philadelphia.
Suri Levow Krieger is a musician, composer, and teacher in Tenafly, N.J.
Martha Liebowitz (Devora) lives and learns Torah in Jerusalem.
Esther Linder lives and learns Hasidism in Jerusalem.
Pnina Rivka Peli of Jerusalem learns Kabbalah and advocates for women's rights in Israel.
Judy Petsonk is a journalist who lives in Philadelphia.
Carol Rose (Atara) is a writer who both teaches women's studies courses and trains day care workers in Winnipeg, Canada.
Teresa Terrell (Tamar) is a social worker who is active in B'nai Brith Hillel at Indiana University, Bloomington.

*   *   *

The women's *Rosh Hodesh* groups of Philadelphia, Jerusalem, New York, and Boston along with *B'not Esh* have provided the evolving ritual context in which my work was able to flower.

Ellen Stone of *Genesis 2*, the innovative Jewish newspaper of Boston, published earlier versions of several chapters (March/April 1983-February/March 1984) and encouraged me to write this book.

Selma Williams and Rabbi Everett Gendler were kind enough to read and critique the manuscript.

My husband, Steven, was the generous patron of this work and constant challenger of my ideas.

Special thanks also go to Martha Ackelsberg, Edith Benjamin, Ruth Fingerhut, Benji Jackson, Carl Perkins, Drorah Setel, Marcia Spiegel, Sheila Peltz Weinberg and Janet Zimmern-Kahan for their help.

Appreciation is expressed to Havurat Shalom of Somerville, Ma. for the use of their building for a photo session.

Finally, my editor, Doris B. Gold, gave invaluable guidance, vision, and enthusiasm to *Miriam's Well* and taught me how to be patient through all the stages of creating a book.

MIRIAM'S WELL

CONTENTS

Part I.

Part II.
Rituals for Women Around the Jewish Year
(starred months indicate women's life-cycle events)

Part III.

At twilight on the second day of Creation, God embedded a precious liquid jewel in the earth, a miraculous well of pure, sparkling water. From one generation to the next, the well belonged to those who knew how to draw up its water. Filled with *mayim chayim*, living waters, the well was a reminder to all who drank or drew from it, that Torah, the way of the Jewish people, is also a well from which all may drink and be restored.

from the Legend of Miriam's Well*

*See month of *Nisan*.

Many women of all ages are now active in Sabbath and holiday Torah readings in the synagogue.

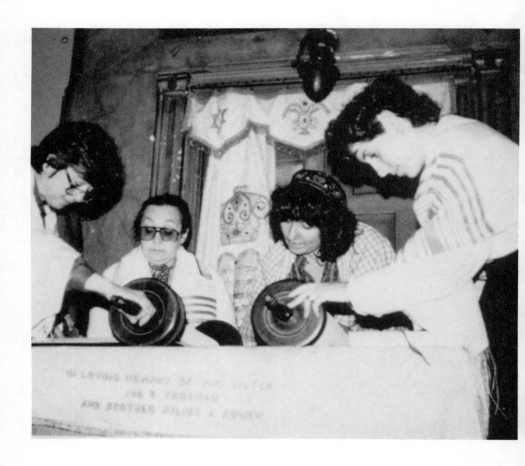

(Photo by Diane Shavulsky-Balestra) National Council of Jewish Women, NY Section, 1984.

PART I.

Sixth century mosaic floor of the Bet Alpha synagogue showing zodiac signs for the month.

THE JEWISH CALENDAR AND ROSH HODESH[1]

Most calendars in use throughout the world are solar, based on the rotation of the earth around the sun. The Jewish calendar, however, is lunar-solar, based on both sun and moon, with months figured on the phases of the moon, and the year based on the rotation of the earth around the sun, 365 days, compared with moon days calculated at 354 days. This arithmetical "compromise" which leaves 11 days unaccounted for each year, is taken up by adding another month during a leap year occurring each second or third year in the Jewish calendar. (In this book, we have provided *Adar Bet,* a second *Adar,* as is customary)

The Jewish calendar is very ancient, dating from our tribal times, and has an interesting history.[2] As early as the 2nd century, C.E., the twelve lunar months were associated with the twelve zodiacal houses, as can be seen from our archeological illustration. This link occurs frequently throughout Jewish art and literature, and thus we include them at the head of each month. The months are associated with the twelve tribes of Israel, their zodiacal signs, twelve parts of the body, twelve archangels and twelve precious stones. While names similar to our Jewish months have been found in Assyrian and Babylonian calendars, their meanings remain unknown.

Rosh Hodesh, the head of the month, is that occasion for special prayers and celebration in the synagogue when the new moon appears, signalling the start of a new month.* It is observed for one or two days. When the latter occurs, the first day is the last day of the preceding month. In the practice of new women's ritual presented in this book, the occasion is marked in settings outside the synagogue with women. In that context, the Jewish calendar becomes a vehicle for noting the monthly cycles of women's fertility and understanding the female aspects of God. Each month bears a seasonal character, a historical and Biblical significance, a sacred quality in its holidays, with new meanings given our female ancestors. The twelve months (and its 13th as well) become analogs to the *sefirot*—emanations of divine being enumerated by the kabbalists. Thus, celebrating *Rosh Hodesh* has become a woman's way to apprehend the *Shekhinah,* the Divine Presence in this world.

Miriam's Well begins with the month of *Tishre* (September/October), since the Jewish New Year begins at Rosh Hashanah, or when the New Moon of Tishre appears.

*See month of Tishre for prayer greeting the new moon.

3

Hebrew Month	Calendar Month	Holidays	Biblical Personalities	Astrological Sign
Tishre	September/ October	Rosh HaShanah Yom Kippur	Dan/Hannah/Peninnah Sarah	Air/Libra Equinox-scale, Venus
Heshvan	October/ November		Gad/Eve/Sarah Rivka	Water/Scorpio Scorpion
Kislev	November/ December	Hanukkah	Tamar/Rachel/Leah Yehudit/Joseph Maccabees	Fire/Sagittarius Archer
Tevet	December/ January	Fast of 10th Day	Naftali/Lilith	Earth/Capricorn Climber
Shvat	January/ February	Tu B'Shvat	Reuven/Miriam Community of Women	Air/Aquarius Water bearer
Adar Aleph (1)	February/ March	—	Ephraim/Menasha Judah	Water/Pisces Fish, mirror image

			Esther/Vashti	
Adar Bet (2)	March/April	Fast of Esther Purim	Esther/Vashti	Water/Pisces Fish, mirror image
Nisan	March/April	Pesah Holocaust	Miriam/Tzipora B'not Yerushalayim B'not zlofchad	Fire/Aries Ram
Iyar	April/May	Lag B'Omer	Issachar	Earth/Taurus Bull
Sivan	May/June	Shavuot	Shimon/Levy Ruth/Naomi	Air/Gemini Twins
Tammuz	June/July	Fast of 17th Day	Zevulun/Great Mother Queen Heaven Astarte/Anat/Tiamat	Water/Cancer Crab
Av	July/August	Tisha B'Av	Judah/Rachel Bat Zion/John	Fire/Leo Lion
Elul	August/September	—	Asher/Bat Sheva Kol Dodi/Virgin	Earth/Virgo Virgin

New Ritual; Ancient Tradition

Miriam's Well is the result of the efforts of Jewish women in the last twenty years to reassess, redefine and recreate their position within religious Judaism. From the 1960's onward, Jewish women in the United States and later in Israel, began forming groups which met in their own homes and focused on a number of areas of concern: prayer, text study, liturgy, ritual and identity. This energy marks a new phase of Jewish female spirituality.

Rosh Hodesh, the monthly holiday marking the new moon, has traditionally been identified with women through *midrash* and folk belief. Therefore, it was a natural vehicle by which these groups could wrestle with the issues they needed to resolve in order to remain active participants in their own heritage. Some groups used a lecture/study format with invited speakers and a designated text; other groups combined improvisational dance, meditation, chanting and creative visualization in their hunger to learn about their female ancestors and role models of the present. What most groups do have in common is a wish to return to traditional sources as a way of reinforcing Jewish identity instead of breaking from it completely. The members of a *Rosh Hodesh* group gain strength from the tradition in grappling with it or integrating it with their new beliefs and practices.

"This Month Is for You," written by Arlene Agus in 1976 in Koltun* was the first step in documenting a particular format for a Rosh Hodesh ritual to be celebrated by women only. Since then, the Jewish Women's Resource Center in New York, and the Women's Institute for Continuing Jewish Education in San Diego, among others, have served as archival and source centers for similar endeavors of contemporary Jewish women.

Miriam's Well: Rituals for Jewish Women Around the Year harks back to the *minhagim* (customs) books which date from the Talmudic era. These books were compilations of the folkways and practices of Jews in communities in Israel and the Diaspora which documented, preserved, and explained *minhagim. Rosh Hodesh* practices vary with each group and each month, but within this multi-colored diversity the theme of the struggle of women within Judaism is woven with one clear thread.

Moon worship was prevalent throughout the ancient Near East.[3] As far back as Biblical times, it is clear that some sort of Festival of the New Moon was celebrated. Eventually, the holiday became the focus of much controversy between the religious establishment and the folk. It was important for the religious leaders to note the needs of the folk who, after all, lived among the other nations of the Near East. Therefore, the New Moon was probably "made" into a *de facto* holiday because people were already designating the advent of the new moon as a sacred time. Stories were circulated about the special right of Jewish women to observe this holiday in recognition of their noble behavior when the Golden Calf was erected and worshipped.[4]

---

*Full citations are given in the Bibliography beginning p. 112.

As a reward for (the women's refusal to participate in the making of the Golden Calf), God gave the new moons as holidays to women, and in the future world too they will be rewarded for their firm faith in God, in that, like the new moons, they too, may monthly be rejuvenated.[5]

As it evolved, the holiday became a way for the religious establishment to combat idol worship and to satisfy the need to continue observance of the sacred relationship between the moon and women which had been part of the indigenous mythologies of the region.

Women were supposed to refrain from work on *Rosh Hodesh,* to eat festive meals, to light candles (a way of commemorating the torches originally lit when the new moon was first sighted in the sky).

Today *Rosh Hodesh* continues to be also marked in the synagogue with special prayers and blessings. It has evolved into a day that is special, not only to women, but to both sexes, as are the Sabbath and other holy days. With the resurgence of feminism in the 1960's, the festival has been moving back again to its original position, that of a sacred time for women.

I am often asked if the *Rosh Hodesh* phenomenon is "really Jewish" or whether it belongs to the long line of pagan practices which the rabbis outlawed. (Frequently the questioner has in mind witchcraft. In every era some women seem to threaten society with their independent and often revolutionary ways. The "witches" of the Middle Ages were merely women who were healers, teachers, non-conformists—those who miraculously survived the Black Death; widows, childless women or single women.)

In today's society, those people who have expressed no sexual preference for the opposite sex are perceived to be as threatening as "witches," becoming as homosexuals the current scapegoats of society. Further, despite the homophobia within Judaism, there is a long and honored tradition of Jewish men praying, learning, dancing and singing together. Only recently have Jewish women attempted to forge their own communal way of worship. The *Rosh Hodesh* festival is one such way.

Rosh Hodesh groups appeal to all women who have felt disenfranchised from their heritage—orthodox and liberal women, Lesbian and straight women, young and old women. *Rosh Hodesh* has become a sacred time for women. Separated from the usual mixed male and female society, women feel free to take on the task of reinterpreting and refining language, ritual, sacred symbol and story so that they can feel at one with their own authentic traditions. Sexual preference becomes simply another orientation in discussion and celebration. For some Jewish Lesbians, marking significant times in the Jewish life cycle and Jewish year together with other women is a way to instill new meaning into their Judaism. The same holds true for heterosexual women. In the *Rosh Hodesh* group, the boundaries between women which operate in society are no longer so sharply felt, because we no longer act in reaction to society but in freedom from it.

Sharing the same sexual orientation, therefore, is not crucial for women sharing womanspace; but being of the same sex does produce a sense of togetherness in our perception of being excluded from our own tradition and of possessing powers which men (and even women) fear. Besides our common gender, we share a common mythic foundation. At Purim, those who dress up as Queen Esther or parade about as Queen Vashti, share a tradition passed down from grandmother to mother to daughter. This too is part of the collective myth assumed by participants.

Miriam's Well illustrates the process of mythmaking in a Jewish women's group—the continuing practice of adding to the story of a people. Ultimately, this can include women and men together.

The Creative Process of Rosh Hodesh

The group process required for creative ritual is the very essence of the *Rosh Hodesh* experience.

To live meaningfully as women and as Jews in the latter half of the twentieth century, in the fifty-eighth century of the Jewish calendar, we need to learn how to do what the rabbis have always done—to seek the deeper meanings of our sacred texts. We have done this through storytelling, singing, dancing and eating the special foods based on our "text," i.e., the month we are marking.[6] Many have turned for inspiration of rituals to the Torah, embedded there like hidden jewels; old/new forms which have added meaning to our lives.

Mostly we have sought to understand our tradition and the unique role of women within it by telling our life stories and the tales of women in the Bible, of women in Jewish history, of women in our own families. As Barbara Myerhoff, noted Jewish anthropologist, said of her grandmother, "Sofie knew and taught me that everyone had some story . . . Stories told to oneself or others could transform the world."[7]

The women who are little-known such as Judith in the *Apocrypha*, Lilith in the *Alphabet of Ben Sira*, Tamar in Genesis 38, and Keturah in Genesis 25, have stimulated our imaginations as much or even more than the giants—Deborah, Esther, Sarah, Eve. So little has been written about this first group that we have been free to ask, explore, fantasize, create. Study of the Torah and its commentaries has fortified us in our quest for understanding. An example:

One year when the Torah portion *"VaYishlach"* (Genesis 32:4-36:43) was being read, Cynthia, a member of the Philadelphia Rosh Hodesh group heard this as part of the discussion of the text. The man leading the discussion quoted: "And it came to pass, when she (Rachel) was in hard labor, that the midwife said to her: Fear not; you shall have this son also."[8] He told us that the Midrash explains this puzzling sentence, 'you shall have this son also' as a reference to the accepted notion that "with every tribal ancestor a twin sister was born, but with Benjamin an additional two twin sisters were born."[9] This makes thirteen sisters in all.

Cynthia told us no further information about these thirteen sisters, but the same fragment was repeated in different texts. She questioned aloud for other details: the names of the sisters; why no one had mentioned this before, etc. When Cynthia shared this find with the group, our imagination responded instantly. Perhaps, we thought, there had been a scroll written by one or more of them . . . or that the scroll was another version of the Torah—the Law received as a woman, lost in the desert wanderings of the Israelites. Or it may never have been recorded and could have become a portion of the Oral Law* forgotten entirely or excluded from the Talmud. The only vestige remaining today is this verse in the *Midrash* about the thirteen twin sisters of the twelve tribes.[10]

The lost scroll of the thirteen sisters has become a *tabula rasa* on which to write the stories, past, present, and future of Jewish women. This scroll has taken shape as **Miriam's Well.** The women who observe *Rosh Hodesh* think of it as a book of recipes, one for each month, one for each sister. The thirteen sisters have come to symbolize the thirteen (cyclical) moons of the Jewish year.[11] As with most recipes, the intention is to inspire the use to create new rituals which answer the needs of a specific group, instead of following ours to the letter.

Many of the rituals in these pages have to do with bodily functions—first menstruation, pregnancy, childbirth, menopause. This is a response to the traditional and problematic Jewish attitude towards women and their bodies.

Women are considered to be *gashmiut;* earthy and tactile beings, restricted by their bodies which change every month like the moon. Hence, they are perceived by the tradition to be volatile; unstable. The mythical figure, Lilith exhibits such behavior in the extreme. In contrast, men are considered to be *ruchniut,* spiritual and heavenly beings. We have sought to integrate the human body into the Jewish rituals which follow.

At this juncture in modern Western Jewish worship, we are as removed as possible from body or earth awareness. As Jewish women, we have no desire to return to the oppressive conditions of our female ancestors whose lives revolved around key points in the lifecycle (menstruation, pregnancy, birth, menopause) to the exclusion of other aspects of their development.

Just as the abused earth begs to be respected and cherished, so do our bodies. Our challenge is to become aware of our bodies without idolizing them; to discern transcendent meanings in our physicality without bypassing its blood, sweat and tears. The kind of "liberation" which means achieving and expressing one's essential human qualities must encompass a celebration of our bodies, female and male. By learning to celebrate the female body, we shall be able to appreciate the male body as well. In the past, the Torah has received much of men's creative energy: during daily worship and Sabbath services, during the holidays—especially at *Simchat Torah* when men traditionally dance with the sacred scroll and are symbolically married to Her (Torah is of the feminine gender in Hebrew).

In the context of *Rosh Hodesh,* Jewish women have begun to foster positive images of the female body by celebrating a young girl's first menstrual period in addition to her bat mitzvah, by creating rituals for pregnancy

*Commentaries on this Torah circulated by word of mouth together with the sacred text were eventually codified as the Talmud.

and pregnancy loss, by marking menopause in a way that is appropriate to each individual. In addition, Jewish women are cultivating positive self-images which will enable them to transcend that which differentiates them from Jewish men and to explore the ultimate goal of the spiritual exercise of *Rosh Hodesh* and Judaism: to explore what it means to be fully *human*.

The creative process of the *Rosh Hodesh* ritual has enabled Jewish women to grow within an ancient heritage which has often felt oppressive and exclusionary. Rediscovering the New Moon as a source of monthly renewal has fulfilled the prophecy of the *midrash* when it explains why *Rosh Hodesh* was given to women.

A PERSONAL PARABLE

In Philadelphia, 1978, thirteen women sat around a table in a *sukkah* in the courtyard of an old apartment building. Our hostess was Aviva, a scholar and perpetual teacher.* She had invited a few friends for a "women's night in the *sukkah.*" She explained that this was *Simchat Beit HaSho'eva,* the second night of *Sukkot.*[12]

At the time of the Great Temple of Jerusalem, in anticipation of winter rains, men and women marked *Simchat Beit HaSho'eva,* the Festival of Drawing Water. One year festivities reached orgiastic heights and ever since, men and women have been separated during prayer in traditional synagogues.[13] Aviva therefore deemed this night appropriate for a "women's night in the *sukkah.*" Since hospitality is a special *mitzvah* of *Sukkot,*[14] she suggested we call on our illuminous female ancestors and invite them too.

Thus began the first Jewish women's ritual I had ever attended, the first time in my 25 years that I was at a meal whose express purpose was to share an occasion to honor our women ancestors.

We all agreed that Miriam, the prophetess, should be invited first. "She is such an expert in celebrations," Aviva noted. "After all, she was the one who thought to remind the women to bring their musical instruments when they were hurrying out of Egypt."

"Let's hold hands round the table," proposed our hostess and, continuing in a calm, soothing voice, "Now close your eyes and imagine Miriam with her bells and tambourine."

The bells chimed, the tambourine jangled and when we opened our eyes again, Miriam seemed to be sitting with us at the table with a place set before her. Dressed in loose, flowing robes the colors of desert sands, she wore no veil, being among women. Her eyes glinted black onyx, reflecting the still-welcome heat of the sun just after dawn. We awaited her words.

"I have brought you a gift, my women friends, since you have invited me to celebrate the fruits of your harvest with you. Do you know how long it has been since anybody thought to invite me into the *sukkah?* My brothers, Moses and Aaron, are always being asked, but not I.

"In gratitude for such long-awaited hospitality, I give you these." She opened her hands which had been clasped together, palm to palm, as if she were opening up a sacred book. Hebrew letters sparkled like diamonds and rubies. We drew breath sharply at seeing such precious jewels up close.

Miriam carefully placed the letters on the table before us. Shimmering, they formed the words—*Be'er Miriam,* the Well of Miriam.

"Behold these letters a moment. Then close your eyes. Each of you will see something—a vision of the Well. Share what you see with each other."

As she instructed, we fixed on the glistening letters for some time, then closed our eyes.

*See Addenda, Part I. p. 111.

Who could say how much time passed? Each of us lapsed into a deep reverie, brought on by the rare beauty of those letters. When we awoke, Miriam was absent and the Hebrew letters had vanished.

We each wanted to know what the others had imagined. Around the circle we told of our visions.

Aviva began: "I was sitting at this well and I had the sense that others had dipped into it before me. Although I could not see them, I felt their presence. A very peaceful feeling."

Next was Tamar who had recently converted to Judaism. "I saw my old well where I was used to drawing water all dried up and empty. So I wandered until I heard a voice from heaven, a *bat kol*. The voice directed me to a new and bountiful supply of water."

Sitting next to Tamar was Sheila who said, "The well I saw contained the depths of sadness and pain, the way I felt when I lost my child. Then I saw people come to fill containers full of water for their gardens. When they sprinkled the water over the earth, flowers bloomed everywhere. As the Psalmist says, "Those who sow in tears will reap in joy."

Then Liba spoke, "I heard an old man at a well singing a song with his children, a song from his youth in Poland before the war. He had long since forgotten this song, all about drawing the water up from a well. Like a miracle, he heard his own children singing this very song to the well as they waited to cast down their buckets. The old man recalled it once more and sang with them."

When Liba had finished, Suri said, "The well I saw issued forth the songs my mother sang. My own voice and my mother's voice arise from those depths."

Devora's turn was next. "In great thirst, I sat by the well for a long while, waiting for someone to come because I had no bucket, no cup of my own. Then Rebecca, Isaac's wife-to-be, came along and drew water for me without my even asking."

Maia, whose name means "water" in Arabic, said, "I asked Miriam, herself, if she would teach me how to sing to the well. You see, my mother died when I was young, before she could teach me how to sing. Miriam took my hand and we danced around the well together. Joy surged through me and poured out of my mouth in full song."

Atara spoke: "I saw the well become a womb, deep and full and endless. My creativity comes from this womb, from the womb of imagination."

Esther was next. "I saw my mother at the well, trying to draw up the water. But she wasn't strong enough to pull up the full bucket and so I had to help her. But then, I had no cup with which to drink and so she offered me hers."

Kokhava: "It was the day I got my first period. The blood made me afraid, even though I had been told it would happen. I cried my tears filling the well until they brimmed over the top, spilling over me. When I bathed in their waters, I stopped crying. Then, miraculously, energy surged through me, the strength of all the tears I had wept. I thought of my grandmother who used to say, "I've cried so many tears that ships could sail on them."

Pnina Rivka: "I looked straight down into the well but could not see through that darkness. I knew something very important was hidden way down there and that I would have to continue to search and not despair."

Lynn Miriam: "It was the day before my wedding. The well invited me to purify myself in its fresh and living waters, as in a *mikveh,* to cleanse myself of my old life in order to embrace my new one."

Finally, my turn came: "In my vision, I saw the well surrounded by a dancing, singing circle of women and men. When they grew thirsty, they gave each other drink from the well's waters, when tired, they bathed each other in the living waters. All the while, the waters were rejoicing upward to the well's very brim."

When we had all shared what we had seen, Aviva poured a glass of water for each of us. "Let's drink to Miriam!" she exclaimed. We drank, savoring the sublime taste of water which had been graced by her presence.

The Re-Creation of a Ritual

Conversation was different that night in the *sukkah,* different from talk with women when men are present, different from talk between men and women in general. Words flowed like water among women who were meeting for the first time with a sacred purpose: to invite our noble ancestors into the *sukkah.* Therefore, our words were infused with sacredness, too.[15] As we brought in Devorah, the judge, and Miriam, the prophetess, and Esther, the queen to celebrate with us, their spirits brought into the *sukkah* laughter and learning.

As each of us took turns doing the inviting, we explained the reasons for our choice, citing each woman's merits and indicating her unique place in our history. Not all were Biblical heroines or famous figures; some were relatives or teachers who had lived in other times and places. The purpose in opening the *sukkah* to our foremothers was to welcome them, at last, into this place to which their husbands alone had always been invited. This was our chance to rectify our centuries-old exclusion.

Thus, as we included our female ancestors, we brought in more of ourselves, too—our intimate thoughts and feelings about being women and Jewish, subjects which seldom found space in daily conversation but which found here a welcome home. For some, "women's night in the *sukkah*" was the first experience with "womanspace," a time and place set aside by women for women only, a concept which Virginia Woolf had described in *A Room of One's Own.*[16]

That *Sukkot* evening as we ate and drank heartily at the same table with the spirits of our foremothers, as we sang songs of harvest and of the fruits of the earth and the womb, as we confessed to the lonely, separate struggles in which we had been engaged, searching for words and ways with which to address *Shekhinah,* the female aspect of God, we laid the foundation for the celebration of *Rosh Hodesh.* Ironically, we were also finding a new, and better meaning of *mehitza,* the separation of men and women at certain specified, sacred times.

By the end of the evening, we had decided to continue our exploration of the possibilities in this voluntary and deliberate monthly separation of women from the rest of the community.

Aviva informed us how some women in the early 1970's had reclaimed *Rosh Hodesh* as their own.[17] "Since I became involved," she said, "I've been making *Rosh Hodesh* each month. When I moved from Minneapolis to Philadelphia, I brought the ritual with me. And that's how it all began."[18]

We did not need to be asked twice. We quickly determined the date of the next new moon and planned to meet again at a different's woman's house. Thus, the first Philadelphia Rosh Hodesh group was born.

Since that time, I have participated in groups in Jerusalem, New York, and Boston. Groups now exist all over the United States and in Israel.

How to Use This Book

In the course of this book, the reader is directed to many "wells"—the Torah and its accompanying written and oral tradition; one's own family history, the stories which forebears have conveyed to offspring, and older Jewish women eager to be mentors on questions reflecting the search for women's wisdom. Especially nourishing have been the rhythms, melodies, patterns and words which flow through each human being, no matter how unskilled; the spiritual and creative lore of people the world over—all offering alternative perspectives to the efforts of Jewish women. Along the way, other "wells" will be found which women never imagined.

In this work we have provided models for creating rituals, but they do not encompass the full range of such activity. The needs and orientation of a specific group determine the flowering of this genre. As an example—no ritual has been presented for divorce or for the end of a relationship between two people. However, two rituals for loss are outlined: one for the loss of a beloved relative or friend (Tevet-December/January) and one for the loss of a pregnancy (Tammuz-June/July). Both serve as models for further rituals.

The creative process of Rosh Hodesh celebrations has resulted in sensitizing Jewish women to the need for communal gatherings marking significant life cycle events when they occur. Our own work focuses on ritual activities appropriate to the context of women-only groups. Thus, standard rituals such as bat mitzvah or girls' baby naming are not documented, only cited.

While we have presented a specific number of ritual activities, we have referred to other possibilities throughout the chapter text and notes. Readers should feel free to use any activity appropriate to the group—i.e., if a woman is to be married in the month of *Shvat* (February/March) instead of *Elul* (August/September) as described in the text, then the themes of *Shvat* such as planting seeds and the advent of Spring can be linked to marriage. The themes and symbols of each month may themselves be variously interpreted according to group members' inclinations. Thus each month can be read as a script to which changes and new directions may be added.

As a major ingredient of *Rosh Hodesh* ritual is storytelling, stories and anecdotes as collected in joint study sessions or interviews have been included here under "Personal Tales." They provide a sense of the oral tradition of Jewish women known from earliest times, as when Lilith commiserated with Eve over their troubles with Adam. As most oral material has been left unwritten, we have recorded some exchanges verbatim, serving as examples of the potential in all of us, realizing that since they were told in the presence of women only, we are providing a link with the past.

Key Terms in MIRIAM'S WELL

kavannah   — The intention or focus of the activity presented.

midrash   — Interpretation of a text; a story or folktale which demon-
                strates an interpretation.*

mikveh   — The ritual bath used in women's purification rites. In
                the context of *Rosh Hodesh,* the mikveh refers to an
                activity in which spiritual purification is the aim; i.e., a
                "mikveh" of song/dance/chant/speech.**

mishkan   — The sanctuary; the portable ark for the Holy of Holies
                which the People Israel used in the wilderness. In the
                context of *Rosh Hodesh,* mishkan refers to the place of
                inner peace unique to each person.

niggun   — A tune without words.***

Shekhinah   — The Indwelling Presence of God which is everywhere;
                in Kabbalistic lore, Shekhinah refers to the feminine
                aspect of the divine.

tikkun   — The repair or healing of the spirit, the planet and the
                universe.

Miriam's Well is best used in conjunction with several basic reference books. See the Bibliography for complete citations. A suggested list follows:

1) Hebrew Bible plus the Apocrypha;

2) Eliahu Kitov's *Book of Our Heritage,* a guide to the months of the Jewish year including their customs, history, stories, and festivals;

3) *Encyclopaedia Judaica;*

4) Siegel, Strassfeld and Strassfeld's *The Jewish Catalog,* a practical introduction to Jewish law and practice;

5) Susan Weidman Schneider's recent *Jewish and Female,* a comprehensive account of the practices and struggles of contemporary Jewish women;

6) Esther Harding's *Women's Mysteries,* a study of the spiritual and psychological connections between the moon and women;

7) Arthur Waskow's *Seasons of Our Year,* an explanation of the Jewish holidays with innovative ways of celebrating them.

*See Part I notes, No. 22, and A Personal Parable.

**See Part I notes, No. 27.

***See Part I notes No. 21.

Miriam, The Prophetess

Rachel

Sarah (middle) bringing Hagar
to Abraham

Deborah, The **Judge**

Judith

Queen Esther (accusing Haman
before King Ahasuerus)

Ruth and Naomi

Penninah, Elkanah and Hannah.

BIBLICAL
WOMEN

in *Rosh Hodesh* Rituals*

*See Part II, Rituals for Women Around the Jewish Year, for specific months where each is mentioned or celebrated.

Vashti

PART II.

Rituals for Women

Around the Jewish Year

TISHRE
SEPTEMBER/OCTOBER
A Time To Heal

Bring: Bibles, Musical Instruments, Fruits, Honey Cake, Round *Hallot.*

Setting: An evening during the Ten Days of *Teshuvah,* Repentance—the period between Rosh Hashanah and Yom Kippur also known as *Yamim Noraim,* the Days of Awe. *Teshuvah* means "turning around." This time is auspicious for changing the direction of one's life. There are two Keepers of *Tishre,* one male and one female. (In the months that follow there is only one) The Keepers share responsibility for facilitating the group's activities for the first *Rosh Hodesh* of the New Year. In the home where we meet, the living-room ceiling can be hung with fruits of the Fall harvest: pomegranates, grapes, gourds and apples, like an indoor *sukkah.* White garments can be worn to symbolize purification and renewal. We sit in a circle.

> The Keepers of *Tishre* introduce themselves, telling how they came to the group. Each man and woman is invited to tell their English and Hebrew names.

Themes for Tishre

Keeper: *Tishre* is brimming with holidays which usher in the New Year.[1] The New Year's activities extend through Yom Kippur, the Day of Atonement, Sukkot, the Harvest Festival and Simhat Torah, Rejoicing with the Torah. All of these holidays mark the initial weeks of the first month of the year.

By Simhat Torah, each of us has made the round of prayer, fasting*, thanksgiving and rejoicing. One has the opportunity to re-enact the period of summation, contemplation, cleansing, and renewal. Tonight we meet as men and women together, going to the Well as a community. Soon comes Yom Kippur, bearing the hint of an ancient custom which used to take place on *Tu B'Av,* the fifteenth of *Av.* On these two days, Yom Kippur and *Tu B'Av,* sex roles were reversed. All the unmarried people gathered in the fields. The women asked the men to dance and then to marry.[2]

We meet together today in hopes of questioning and challenging sex roles which are still alive and often restrain us. In the context of *Rosh Hodesh* as we Jewish women celebrate it here, the essence of the New Moon of *Tishre,* i.e., *Rosh HaShanah,* is the mutual understanding and appreciation of the differences between men and women. Achievement of this understanding aids the attempt at *tikkun,* the mending of destructive differences in the world at large.

Signs of the Months

One woman presents a chart she has made which contains the months of the year, their astrological signs, the names of the tribes, biblical figures

---

*See Note for New Year.

and each month's physiological association, with Jewish festivals occurring each month.*

We discuss the Jewish months and astrology, using the chart.

The Jews lived among the renowned astrologers of ancient times—Egyptians, Babylonians and Greeks. The Talmud includes several full-blown astrological systems, one for determining the hours of the day which are ruled by the various planets and another that suggests the personality types born on different days of the week. However, the main interest in sky-watching expressed in rabbinic literature is directed to the proper setting of festival dates and the appreciation of planetary cycles as the handiwork of God. Still, many suffering Jews in Christian Europe tried to determine the time of the Messiah's arrival through astrology. As far back as the second century C.E., the twelve lunar months of the Jewish calendar were associated with the twelve zodiacal houses. This is evident from the beautiful mosaic floor of the ancient synagogue at Beit Alpha.[3]

Sign of Tishre

Man: The astrological sign of Tishre is *Moznayim,* Scales. The year reaches equilibrium here, at the point where heat turns to cold, Summer turns to Fall, and the old year gives way to the new. Rosh HaShanah is the annual day of judgment. The scales are the Scales of Justice. God weighs good deeds against evil ones and determines "who shall live and who shall die."[4]

This is also the time when the masculine/active/aggressive, and feminine/passive/receptive energies in the universe will unite to form an even greater power. The Chinese call these two streams in dynamic opposition to each other, Yin and Yang. We recognize this duality and name God in different ways—*Adonai,* Lord, for example, representing the masculine; and *Shekhinah,*, Indwelling Presence, representing the feminine.[5] The scales of *Tishre* imply a balance; men and women together developing their full potential in the context of Jewish tradition. This is perceived as a unifying force strengthening the universe.

Storytelling

Now a man reads aloud in Genesis 1:14-19, about the creation of the sun and moon.

A woman then tells a *midrash* which responds to the sages' question: "Why is the moon's light less bright than that of the sun?"

THE LIGHT OF THE MOON

At the beginning of Time, God created light so that the whole of Creation could be visible. God made the light of the sun and the moon exactly equal in intensity.

The moon could not understand God's reason for equalizing the glow of the two heavenly bodies and asked, "How can both of us merit the same amount of light?" God answered by

*See illustration in Part I.

decreasing the moon's light to a milky-white glow and keeping the silent sun's light as strong as before.

Then the moon protested. "But God, is it fair that I should be punished for speaking up?"

God conceded the point and granted that Israel would mark the months of the year as each new moon appeared. Even more, in the world to come, God promised that the moon would be restored to its original light and be as powerful as the sun.[6]

Now we discuss this imaginative *midrash*. One participant with a scientific bent explains the relationship between the earth and moon as planets revolving around the sun, receiving its light. Then we tell incidents from our lives associated with the moon. Two follow:

Woman: One night I was walking by myself in Jerusalem. I wasn't completely alone because the moon shone and was full. She was so close I felt I could touch her. I kept running down the streets of the Holy City, trying to come closer. As I did I was puzzled. The moon seemed to be challenging me, asking: "Do you really know what I am? Am I so passive? Am I so accepting? Don't I have my own powers to offer? Do you want to know what they are?"

The moon seemed to say, "**I can be big, bright and light. I can be far away, I can be distant and hidden behind the clouds. I can come very close to the earth when I want to be involved with life.**"

I remembered then how the life of the moon is linked to the ocean tides, how it is often reflected in the water, showing a particular attachment to earth, as if a reunion were happening with the moon and the earth, with the moon and the sun, with male and female.

That night when I seemed so close to the moon, I sensed that her longings were mine as well. The moon wants to be restored to her original light; to be as bright as the sun with a different quality to her light. She wants to be loving and giving, to have empathy and understanding for all creatures. She also wants to act with strength based on her convictions, to be proud of her beliefs.

How will this occur? The moon will have to find her own way; she could become proud, free and confident. She can exude strength and beauty in her own way, not in isolation, but with the joy of taking and receiving strength.

I see her now with great hope. The moon belongs to the earth and yet is not of the earth. The moon belongs to the sky and yet is not of the sky. The moon is the intermediary body of acceptance and giving. I have much to learn from her.[7]

The women and men react to this story. Some recall their own lunar incidents.

Woman: I remember that as a little girl, I was allowed to accompany my grandfather outdoors at night after the Sabbath was over. He went to stand on a nearby street corner with some other men to recite *birkat halevanah,* the blessing of the New Moon. I noticed each man lifted a finger to point to the pale crescent in the sky when it came into view. Then all quickly turned their backs on the moon as they recited the blessing.

As we walked home, I asked my grandfather the reason for the men turning their backs. He said, "To look at the moon as we make the blessing would be *avodah zarah,* idol worship. Avraham *Avinu,* our father, taught that we must turn our backs on this."

"But won't the Moon's feelings be hurt?" I childishly asked.

"The Moon has no feelings," said my grandfather. "Only God and man have feelings."

His answer never satisfied me. Even if the moon had no feelings, didn't she sense that we were turning our backs on her? What if she decided not to show up in the sky some night because we were being so rude? I have inherited my grandfather's horror of idol worship, but have still never been comfortable with turning my back on the moon.[8]

Discussion of this controversial topic of marking the New Moon and the potential for idol worship follows.

Music: The group sings songs of light: "Or Zarua LaTzaddik," traditional Jewish liturgy; also "This Little Light of Mine," traditional spiritual, and "Moonshadow."[9]

Blessings: We chant together original blessings for the New Moon and New Year.

BLESSING FOR THE NEW MOON[10]

All: Shekhinah, Presence of Blessing,
       We rejoice in Your cycles of renewal.

       May it be your will,
       Life-Spirit of our Mothers,
       To increase the brilliance of the moon
       So that it may no longer be reduced in size;

       May the light of the moon again be like the light of the sun,
       As it was during the first days of Creation,
       For it is said, "The two great lights."[11]
       May this promise be realized in our days through us and our actions.

       Brukhah At Shekhinah Mehadeshet Hodashim.

       Shekhinah, Presence of Blessing,
       You bring constant renewal.

BLESSING FOR THE NEW MOON AND NEW YEAR[12]

All: Eloheinu v'Elohei Avoteinu v'Imoteinu Hadesh Aleinu Hodesh Zeh v'Shanah Zot

       Dear God, God of our Mothers and Fathers
       Renew us this month and this year
       Direct us
       Toward goodness and blessing
       Toward the joyful
       Toward liberation and challenge, as well as
       Toward patience and consolation
       Toward becoming ever more human beings.
       Let us become capable of supporting ourselves,
       Our families and friends,
       Let us serve our community in dignity.

       Direct us
       Toward life and peace
       Toward observing our blindness

Toward struggling with our goals
Toward forgiving ourselves and each other.

You chose us with an intention
You gave us the awareness of the cycles of the moon.
May we use this gift as an opportunity to understand what you intend
for us.
Thank you—for inviting us to share your holiness and
This holy moment of the New Year.

Since we are celebrating the Creation of the world, it is appropriate to study a portion of the story of the Creation from the Torah. We choose to study the creation of the first man and first woman. (You may study whatever portion of the story is most pertinent to your group)

Keeper: Let's read in Genesis 2:5 through 3:24, the account of the creation of man and woman. The men will read Adam's lines aloud in unison. The women will read Eve's lines. All will read the lines about God and the serpent.

After the reading we discuss the story and the issues it raises. Here are some sample questions. (Each group should generate its own)

—What is the meaning of Adam's being created from the earth in view of "adama" being the word for "earth" in Hebrew?

—What is the meaning, symbolic or real, of Eve's being "born" of Adam?

—What are the parallels between this story and the *midrash* of Sun and Moon we have presented here?

—What do we learn about sex differences from this story?

Woman: I'd like to tell the story of Lilith who was Adam's wife *before* Eve. This is a *midrash* on the Creation story, an echo of the legend which explains the inequality of the sun and moon, a response to the question: Why wasn't Eve created from the dust of the earth as was Adam?

LILITH

The first woman was named Lilith, meaning "Night Being." Like Adam, she was created from the dust of the earth. Since they were of equal origin, Lilith felt completely justified in refusing to lie beneath Adam when they made love.

But Adam could not tolerate this. He complained to his Creator, "What kind of woman have you made for me? She refused to do as I say."

By this time Lilith had left Adam. She had simply uttered the secret name of God and then flown away.

God sent three angels after her, to ask if she would comply with her husband's needs and return to him. The angels told her that if she refused to come back, hundreds of her children would be drowned in the Sea of Reeds every day.

Lilith did not have to deliberate long before making her decision—she chose never to return to Adam.[13]

We discuss the Lilith story.
Keeper: The story of Lilith underlines the main purpose of tonight's meeting: better communication between the sexes.

For me the *tikkun* needed to be made between men and women is for us to be able to speak to each other in our *own voices*. That means first finding the "voice" or form of expression, unhampered by expectations or fear of what the other will "think" or "feel" about the value or authenticity of that voice. Perhaps that's why women have chosen to explore and develop that "voice" in small groups with other women to strengthen themselves. Now many of us are ready to use that voice in the world.[14]

As an introduction to sharing that "voice" together, we'd like to focus on the imagery of the Garden of Eden.

Guided Imagery: Garden of Eden[15]

Woman: We begin by singing a *niggun* for several minutes. Keep singing and begin to notice your breathing. Now gradually stop singing and focus on your breath as it goes in and out, in and out, in and out. . . .

Imagine you are in the Garden of Eden . . . as Adam or Eve. You don't have to be Adam if you're male or Eve if you're female. Just be whoever you want to be.

Feel yourself in the Garden. What does it look like? Smell like? Sound like?

How do you relate to your partner? See yourself interacting with him or her . . . And just be there in the Garden of Eden. . . . When distracting thoughts enter, just go back to your breathing. Focus on that for a while. . . .

Now, imagine you've just eaten some of the forbidden fruit of the Tree of Knowledge. How does the fruit taste? Does the fruit give you a new thought? What can you see or feel now? Is it different from before?

Now, begin to describe this experience to your partner in the Garden. Use words, gestures or facial expressions.

Now, do the opposite. If you have been Eve, become Adam; if Adam, become Eve. Experience again the tasting, etc.

Is it different? Say how. Try to feel this difference. Imagine explaining this difference to your partner.

"Switching" like this may bring insight you never had before. Hold this insight inside you like a child in the womb of your understanding. This child is the Messiah you will bring into the world.

When you're ready, you may open your eyes.

Now, if you wish, turn to the person of the opposite sex nearest you and share whatever you wish.

Think if men and women and women can provide each other a vessel for dipping into Miriam's Well, they may learn how to express their unique visions of the world to each other.

Tashlikh/Ritual of Cleansing:
Keeper of **Tishre:** Now, let's end with a short ritual of purification. In this way we shall enter the New Year free of the impediments of the last one. We are constantly being renewed throughout the Jewish year—at Purim, at Pesach,

at *Tisha B'Av.* The renewal of *Rosh HaShanah* marks the beginning of the entire world.

Tashlikh usually takes place in the afternoon of the first day of Rosh HaShanah. People go to the nearest moving body of water: a stream, river, or ocean, and empty their pockets into the water, symbolically discarding their sins.

Water is the medium of "cleansing" for several reasons. *Mayim chayyim,* living water, is a purifying agent. Also, fish live in water. The ever-open eyes of fish recall the all-seeing eye of God which beholds the wrongdoings of men and women and offers forgiveness when they are revealed.[16]

As we walk to the water, we turn our pockets inside out. Think about what you need to purge in yourself.

The Keeper leads the group to the closest body of moving water.

Keeper: Since our *kavannah* for this *Rosh Hodesh HaHodshim,* the first New Moon of the year, has been to heal some of the wounds in the relationships between the sexes, I would like to toss away the obstacles of my own making which stand in the way of expressing myself honestly before the opposite sex.

Those who feel so moved now speak about what they would like to remove from their lives in this context. They also empty their pockets into the water.

We remain outdoors and now we sing songs for the New Year, using our musical instruments—flutes, drums, bells, sticks, guitars. Some play music, *Hashiveinu* (Jewish Liturgy) "Return Again",[17] "Turn, Turn, Turn"[18] and some dance. There are circle dances, circles of men, circles of women, circles of men and women.

Exhausted and exhilarated, we consume a feast of harvest fruits and round *hallot,* honey cake and sweet wine.

HESHVAN
OCTOBER/NOVEMBER
A Time To Seek

Bring: Blankets; pumpkins, gourds, Fall flowers; hot mulled cider; Indian Pudding; Zucchini Bread, other harvest foods.

Setting: An autumn evening. We are sitting in a circle at the home of the month's Keeper (preferably a woman who has marked Rosh Hodesh before). Blankets are placed for seats, or for wrapping, as wanted.
The New Year in Israel arrives during our U.S. summer. We know our Fall has arrived in the Northeast by the pumpkins, gourds, etc. showing the passing of the year's harvest. The growing season in Israel and other lands leapfrog each other. In the Holy Land, the last full burst of roses, grapes and pomegranates gives way to the welcome drone of winter rain. In some parts of the USA this also occurs, but our summer grows lush and green. Heshvan often jolts us into awareness of winter and inward turning.

Themes for Heshvan: This month is often called *Mar Heshvan,* ("Mar" means a "drop of water.") According to Genesis, the Deluge occurred this month and thus becomes a time of tragedy. A second meaning of Mar Heshvan is "the bitterness of Heshvan," so-called because there are no holidays or festivals to make the month a "sweet" one, such as Tishre (September/October) which has many festivals.[1]

Sign of Heshvan: *Akrav,,* the Scorpion, lends another clue to the essence of Heshvan. This animal burrows deep into the earth, waiting to sting its prey. In the same way we penetrate the depths of our own psyches before returning to the light. In this period just before winter, we become introspective in preparation for the Spring re-emergence. It is a time for recapitulating ourselves and understanding our origins.
A story which illustrates this time of inward seeking is the Greek myth of Amor and Psyche.[2]

Introductions:
Keeper: This is the month when we really mark Rosh Hodesh as a women-only holiday. At Tishre we met together with the men to start the Jewish New Year. Each year at Heshvan, we return to a group slightly different from that of the last. For some of us, this is a first time; for others it is the first time with this group, so we shall introduce ourselves, giving our Hebrew names, their meanings, and tell something about our namesake. Then we'll speak about ourselves and how we came to women's ritual:

Aviva: I'm Aviva, which means Spring. It's my fifth season of celebrating Rosh Hodesh—in Philadelphia, Jerusalem, and now here. (She describes her first encounter with the ritual and her views about a special holiday for Jewish women)[3]

26

Atara: My name is Atara, which means "crown." I've known Aviva for many years, sharing the same questions and problems. I'm glad to be here tonight.

Perla: My name is Perla, Pearl in Yiddish. I was named for my great-grandmother on my mother's side. I came to the group because of a dream I had last year, directing me to act. When Suri told me about this group, I decided I had to come, so here I am.

(She is asked to tell about her dream by the women. She responds)

In the dream I'm sitting at my grandfather's deathbed. The dark room smells as musty as his bathrobe hanging from a hook on the door. There is one window, shut tight; very little light; hardly any air, but I don't feel stifled. The only sound I hear is the clock ticking on a table. My hand is curled around my grandfather's as he breathes irregularly. I feel his blood trying to meet mine through the skin. He is trying hard to hold onto life the way he must have known it, and I seek him sinking before me with a heavy burden, but I feel helpless to save him. I also feel relieved that he is going . . . all that rich and ancient life dissolving like yellowed lace in water. This must be what happens when one gives way to the next generation.[4]

Liba: I'm Liba. That means *love* in Yiddish. I don't know who I was named for. I'm here because I've always been jealous of Hasidic men and their rebbes, how they form such a tight spiritual network. I bring a longing for such a link among women here.

Sarah: Sarah is my name—the wife of Abraham. It actually means "princess." That has bothered me since I was small. I can't remember a time when I wasn't rebelling against the "Jewish Princess" image—as I always played with boys on my street. I've been looking for a place within Judaism to feel comfortable because I never seem to fit in. Like the Rabbi Nachman tale about the king's son who thought he was a rooster which shows that we can become acceptable Jews without giving up our feminine orientation.[5]

Tamar: I'm Tamar. That means date palm tree. I took this name when I converted to Judaism. I used to be Theresa. The year I went to study in Israel, I used to relish eating fresh dates which I had never tasted. That was the year Perla and I were roommates. She invited me here tonight.

Pnina: My name is Pnina Rivka. Pnina is Pearl in Hebrew, and Rivka or Rebecca, means "mother ewe." I come from a family of many rabbis—my husband, my father, my grandfathers. I have learned much from them, but it never seemed enough. I always had questions they couldn't answer: Why is Torah a word in the feminine gender? Why was Eve created from Adam's side instead of the other way around? I often think that asking the right questions is more important than having the right answers.

Maia: I'm called Maia. My name means different things in different languages. In Arabic, it's water; in Indian—illusion; in Russian—mine. I don't have a Hebrew name. Being here tonight is the fulfillment of a legend I grew

up with. My father loves to sing. He gave me a desire to carry on a musical
tradition . . . even telling me I was responsible for finishing Miriam's song.

The song he was referring to is the Song of the Sea (Exodus 15:1-19).
That's the song the Children of Israel sang when they had safely crossed over
the Red Sea, leaving Pharaoh and his men to drown behind them. The Torah
recounts the song in its entirety as sung by Moses and the Children of Israel.
Later the Torah tells us, Miriam took up her timbrel and sang this song. However, only the first few lines are given (Exodus 15:20-21).

So the Rabbis asked the question: Why is the Song of Miriam only
partially stated in the Torah? And in the Midrash is found the answer: the
song is incomplete so that future generations will finish it. That is our task.[6]

After all the introductions, the Keeper sings a *niggun* and the women join; the
sound swelling and receding*

Keeper: Each year at Heshvan as the group begins anew, we relate once
again how the festival of *Rosh Hodesh* began. We remind ourselves of the
time sacred to Jewish women and the revival of the ancient festival of the
New Moon. I think it may soon be my turn to offer the next generation my
grandfather's precious burden which I am now learning how to complete.

Storytelling

The Keeper asks one of the "old-timers"** to tell the story.

ORIGINS OF ROSH HODESH[7]

The festival of Rosh Hodesh was born in the desert where no shadows existed to hide
shapes and colors; neither were there many surfaces to muffle sounds. This was a world of no
distinctions between land or sky, wind or air; different from Egypt we had just left.

In our wilderness wandering we learned to speak to the heavens and find answers written
in the shapes of clouds. The rocks taught us to be patient. The scraggly bushes taught us how to
save the rain, embrace the earth. The palm trees clustered together like children around a green
pool, showing us how to join them on our knees to drink the blessed water. The desert sustained
us all with the same umbilical cord.

Is it any wonder that we who had emerged from the Sea of Reeds together into the
wilderness of Sinai all began to live by one rhythm? And is the wonder any greater that the
cycles of the moon reverberated in every woman at the same time, in the same way? As soon as
the moon was born anew in the sky, each woman began to bleed.

Without saying a word to each other, we women knew it was time to separate ourselves
from the men. As if the moon were calling us, we left camp and hiked together to a wadi a
half-day's distance. We moved at night over the rocks, surefooted as the lizards. The moon
guided us to the place, pulling us with her crescent, a white gleaming magnet in the sky.

When we reached the Wadi of the Moon, we lay on the sand, nestling in the rocks still
warm from the daytime sun and fell asleep. That night we all had a similar dream.

*See p.15 for *niggun*.
**a woman who has participated in many Rosh Hodesh gatherings

One woman told it thus: "We were each bathed very carefully in different ways. The moon bathed us with her light. Our mothers soothed us with the lullabies they had sung to us when we were children. We felt purified with a green fragrance which seemed to emanate from the rocks."

When we awoke, rosemary had sprouted overnight beneath us. We rose as in a spell and embraced each other. Then we began to sing.

Our song seemed to make things grow. There were date palms, figs, grapes, olives appearing all at once and in great abundance. From a rock a spring trickled forth.

We remained in that desert garden for a week, receiving strength from the earth by seating ourselves in special postures, bathing in the moonlight by night and resting in the shelter of the largest rocks by day.

Soon our bleeding ceased. We watched the moon swell to fullness. It was time to return to our camp.

There we found the men were panicking. They shouted about being abandoned, first by Moses who had climbed the mountain to talk to God and then by us women who had disappeared without a word.

The men feared they would die of thirst. They demanded all our gold ornaments, intending to make a god out of metal. We refused and felt pity for them. They turned from us without asking where we had been. With Aaron reluctantly guiding them, they built an idol. Soon there stood a calf of gold high on a pedestal, beaming foolishly at the mountain. We began to doubt if our week apart in the moonlight had ever happened.

However, in time, with the reappearance of the new moon, we understood our reward: because we had refused to give our ornaments to make an idol, we would be "reborn" each month.[8] The moon would teach us about the rhythms of the seasons and the months of the year.

Several women with the best memories became the Keepers of the Months, responsible for remembering which songs were sung, which postures were learned, which stories were told, which ripe fruits were eaten, which type of fragrance the rocks emanated in a particular month so that we could tell our daughters and granddaughters in years to come. We chose the twin sister of the head of each tribe for this task, as it is written, "To each and every (head of the) tribe was born a twin sister . . . "[9]

This sacred knowledge probably remained hidden over the centuries. As the Jewish people travelled beyond their desert existence, women began to menstruate on different days, each in her own unique relationship to the moon.

The women at Sinai had taken this eventuality into account. They had prayed to the Shekhinah, Moon of Israel, for guidance. If the sacred knowledge of the months were lost, the Shekhinah let them know that in a future time when women sought this monthly wisdom once again, it would be rediscovered as easily as moving aside a rock to uncover the fragrant plant beneath. Then the ritual would be reinstated through a community of women who remember, as in a distant dream, how the moon once called to them at Sinai.

We are that community.

The women react to the story. They talk about the relationship of moon cycles and the menstrual cycle. They speak of how menstrual blood is associated with pollution and impurity today, where in earlier times (as well as in certain tribal societies) it was linked with power and numen.[10] They wonder about the oral tradition, how women's wisdom has been preserved over the centuries.

Movement Meditation: Desert Beginnings

Let's move now in a way that will increase our understanding of Heshvan, time of origins, of beginnings.

All rise at her suggestion.

Now close your eyes and imagine what it feels like to be in our place of origin, in the wilderness, the *midbar*.

Each woman stands silently in her own desert world. Begin to feel the sun beating down . . . hot desert sun. Keep your eyes closed. Each woman moves as if beneath the heat of an imaginary sun. Keeping your eyes closed, imagine that the sun has set and you are again active in the cool of evening. Make the sound of what you imagine yourself to be as you move.

For a few moments, each woman becomes a different desert creature: blowing, bending, slithering, flying, hissing, creaking, soaring.

Now be still once more under the rising heat of the morning sun. Feel the heat and move into a stillness, a calm which is right for you.

Each group should devise its own movement. Some ideas:
—Using floodlights and large cardboard moon shapes (crescent, half, full) create a moon dance.
—Using props appropriate to various seasons/months, enact the course of the seasons of the year.

We emerge from the "desert" to sit once again in a circle. At this point the Leader may ask if anyone wishes to share how she felt in "the desert." Often, it is just as well *not* to talk about a non-verbal exercise such as this and instead to let the experience remain a non-verbal one. This is up to the discretion of the leader and the needs of the group.

Woman: Let's sing songs of origins, of going back to the beginning. (She begins the round and others join)

Hashivenu Adonai elekha   (Return us, God, to you)
V'nashuva   (And we shall return)
Hadesh yameinu k'kedem   (Renew our days as of old)
(Traditional, Jewish liturgy)
We sing other Circle songs:

Turn, turn, turn,[11] I circle Around[12] Circle Game[13] and songs of the coming winter: Urge for Going[14]
All drink hot cider and eat the pudding and breads before ending.

KISLEV
NOVEMBER/DECEMBER
A Time To Be Silent
A Time To Speak

Bring: *Menorot,* salty cheeses, candles, wine.

Setting: A winter evening. We sit on pillows in the living room of the woman who is tonight's host. If there is a fireplace, so much the better. Each woman has brought a menorah.* They are placed on trays in the middle of our circle.

Themes for Kislev

Keeper: I'm glad all could come. Usually we meet on *Rosh Hodesh,* but tonight we meet during Hanukkah. Tonight we've prepared a feast for *Yehudit*—Judith. This is a tradition we've received from the Oriental Jewish women's community. On the seventh night of Hanukkah, they remember the bravery of Judith by having a *Hag HaBanot,* a women's holiday.

Although we rarely hear of Judith, she is credited, along with the Maccabees, for being responsible for the miracle of Hanukkah.[1] Judith and her courageous story represent a new "source of water" in Miriam's Well available to us. She is one of many Jewish women from our past: Deborah, the Judge, and Beruriah, the sage, are two others who have often been neglected. In the month of Kislev, we choose to bring these women out of the darkness into the light so that we can learn from them. We shall tell their stories and sing their praises. (Each women's group may have its own list of women to honor at *Hag HaBanot,* those they consider to be "the strong women" in their national and personal histories.)[2]

Sign of Kislev

This month's sign of the *Keshet,* the Bow, reminds us of the root of Torah which is *yud-resh-heh* and means "to shoot." In Hebrew, the words for parents, *horim,* and teacher, *moreh,* come from this same root.[3] Parents and teachers are the ones who show one how to aim. In *Kislev* we learn how to aim, find the light or unearth the hidden wellspring.

> A woman is asked to tell the story of Judith. She tells the story in her own words, or it can be read aloud from the *Book of Judith* in the *Apocrypha.*[4] We then discuss the questions it stimulates. Some of them follow.
> —How can we revere a woman who killed a man in order to save her people?
> Is the story of Judith appropriate for Hanukkah? Why or why not?
> —What do you think of Judith's use of womanly wiles to achieve her goal, namely the salvation of the Jews?

Keeper: Judith represents much more than a Hebrew "Calamity Jane." She teaches us the way to fight darkness, a recurrent theme throughout our history. She provides us with one model. Each one of us must decide how we might act in a comparable situation in modern times.

---

*Candlestick

31

Many facets of this story remain hidden on a first reading. Consider the name of Judith's town, Bethulia, literally *bethula,* virgin of *Yah,* a name of God. A town called "Virgin of God." Here "virgin" retains its original sense of unmarried woman. Bethulia, therefore, refers to a woman who was unmarried, yet pledged to God.

Recently widowed, Judith was determined to keep her independence, to be faithful to her deepest values, to God. Of all the men and women in Bethulia, Judith alone conceived a plan to keep the Jews and Israel from having to "marry," to submit to a foreign invader. Only unmarried Judith, fiercely protective of herself and her people, could retaliate successfully. With her feminine beauty and with food, she seduced Holofernes and beheaded him.

> Judith's words delighted Holofernes . . . and they were amazed at her wisdom.[5]

She was a match for him. He was not accustomed to expressing respect to a woman, a new and pleasing sensation.

Judith fortified herself by eating only her own food once she was in enemy territory, adhering strictly to the dietary laws. Each night she bathed in the spring of Bethulia. The Assyrian soldiers had surrounded the town, and blocked the water supply. As Judith was outside Bethulia, she purified herself three times before attempting to slay Holofernes, with the ritual triple immersion as in a *mikveh.*

However, unlike a woman's typical use of the *mikveh,* Judith did not purify herself because she had just menstruated or had sexual intercourse. In the stance of a warrior before battle, she immersed herself.

Woman: I'd like to read a poem I wrote for Judith at the *mikveh.* The rainbow imagery comes from the fact that during *Kislev,* the Great Flood abated. God put a "bow" in the sky, a sign of the covenant with Noah, the promise that the world would never again be destroyed by flood.

SONG OF JUDITH AT THE MIKVEH[6]

In green tiled tub
I poured the oil
Anointing every pore,

I dried myself
Caressing limbs
In towel of indigo,

Then hung my wrap
On azure lines
To dry 'neath orange glow.

My breakfast feast
A blood red treat
Of pomegranate seeds,

Which stained the page
With purple words
As red and blue agreed.

A yellow shawl
Of warming joy
Enfolded me within,

When Noah's bow
Grabbed hold my soul
And danced it 'round again.

A covenant
Renewed itself
This early ninth month morn,

And made me sing
A sister song
To ritual reborn.

Keeper: There is a tradition of chanting hymns and songs in praise of Judith: All the Israelite women came running to see her; they sang her praises, and some of them performed a dance in her honor.[7]
(The women are given copies of a hymn to chant)[8]
(A woman sings a song she has composed in honor of Judith)[9]

Ki im Yehudit bat Merari
For Judith, daughter of Merari

B'yafifya ripatu
Foiled him with her beauty.

Ki simlat almunata pashta
She removed her widow's garments

Larum amelim bi'Yisrael
To raise up the oppressed in Israel.

The women sing the song several times, each time in a different tempo, from joyful to thoughtful. As the song ends, candles are given to each one.

"Women of Light":
Keeper: Women of light appear often in Jewish lore. There was the light of the candles which Sarah lit at the beginning of the Sabbath. By a miracle, the light remained throughout the entire week, glowing in the tent of Abraham and Isaac. When Sarah died, the task of lighting these sacred candles passed into the hands of Rebecca, the wife of Isaac. Because Rebecca was as worthy as Sarah, she caused the light to remain throughout the entire week as had Sarah.[10]

Queen Esther was also a bringer of light. Known as the morning star, *Ayyelet HaShachar,* she was responsible for conveying a bright, rekindled spirit to the Jews after the long night of persecution and suffering.[11] Esther was also identified with the full moon, shining in the midst of darkness. Like the moon, she hid her true identity until the ordained moment of revelation.[12]

Storytelling
Deborah, the Judge, who lived in the 12th century B.C.E., learned the secret of making light as a young girl. This *midrash* is inspired by the question: "What does 'woman of Lappidot' mean?" Some say Deborah was the wife of a man called Lappidot; others say it refers to Deborah in her glory as a "woman of flames." The following is based on the *Book of Judges,* where it is written, "And Deborah, a prophetess, woman of Lappidot, judged Israel at that time."[13]

DEBORAH, WOMAN OF FLAMES[14]
When Deborah was a young girl, she already knew that God intended her to do special things for her people. But she had no idea what they were to be. When she wasn't helping her mother, she went searching for her mission in life.

Of all places she went to look, the marketplace was best. The musty, sweet and tangy smells, the vendors trying to out-shout each other, the people pushing and shoving to find the best buys—all this thrilled her with the promise of unexpected happenings.

One day, in a far corner of the marketplace, in a dilapidated stall, she saw an old woman. Clad in drab rags, the woman sat on a stool with yards of hemp at her feet. She was making wicks for the lamps in the Holy Temple. As she moved her hands, the hemp seemed to leap and dance between her fingers, turning into strands of light. Deborah's heart leaped too, and she thought, "If only I could learn to make light as this woman does, I am sure my purpose in life would be fulfilled.

The old woman agreed to teach Deborah how to make wicks for the lamps in the Holy Temple. The work would be hard, Deborah was warned.

But Deborah persisted. At first the wicks she made barely cast any light at all. Instructing her, the old woman said, "You must allow the light inside your spirit to flow through your fingers and into the hemp itself."

"But how?" Deborah wanted to know.

"When you weave your wick, think of words of Torah, for they carry much light inside them," replied the old woman.

Deborah made ready to weave. She closed her eyes and thought of words which echoed the need of the time, a prayer for peace *hiney ma tov u-mah nayim shevet achim gam yachad**. She fixed her mind on these words until, like ripe pods, they burst forth with light. Pulsing within her and radiating out to her hands and fingers, the light grew in strength and brightness.

The wicks she made then were stronger than the previous ones. The strands appeared to vibrate as if they were the stems of the living plants from which they had sprung. When the old woman touched fire to the wick, the light burned brilliantly, filling the stall in which they sat.

Now that Deborah had mastered this step, she was ready to move on to the next.

She was told, "This time as you weave your wicks, open yourself to the light of God which is all around and has been since the Creation."

"But how?" Deborah wanted to know.

"Close your eyes and let your mind rest until it becomes as quiet as a pool of oil about to be sparked by God. Thoughts and worries will enter your mind and you will feel unequal to the task of bringing peace to your people. You will think of the factions within the tribes, of the strife which beleaguers the nation from within and from without. You will doubt your own abilities to do anything about this. But you will overcome these thoughts and rise above them."

Everything the old woman said came true. As soon as Deborah closed her eyes, she was plagued by thoughts of an insidious nature. She questioned how she would ever be able to conquer all those doubts and become a vessel for divine light.

She trained her mind on "*hiney mah tov*"** again, this time considering the deeper meaning of the words. A calm and a strength flowed from them. She became one with the light permeating the words, until it seemed the entire marketplace and the world beyond were illuminated. As Deborah allowed her hands to do their familiar dance of hemp weaving, the light gathered strength, travelling from her heart throughout her entire body, unleashing the emotion and power she had stored within. Lights of gold and silver and pure white emanated from her and surrounded her as if she, herself, were a flame.

This time the wick was perfect, glowing before fire ever touched it. The old woman looked at Deborah and said, "You have learned all that I have to teach you. Now you will be called a "Woman of Flames." You know the secret of making splendid lights for the Holy

---

*Reaching deeper and deeper meanings of words is an important Jewish value, especially exemplified by the Kabbalists. See Scholem, "The Meaning of the Torah in Jewish Mysticism," in *On the Kabbalah,* especially pp. 57-59.
**"How good it is for people to live in peace."

Temple. Let the light inside you illuminate all you do. Let the light bring your vision of peace into being."

Indeed Deborah's light continued to grow as she did. Deborah became a woman of importance, a prophetess, a woman of flames. She judged Israel in ancient days, bringing peace to her people and her land.

Keeper: We've now heard about Women of Light; of Judith, Sarah, Esther and Deborah. Now let's light candles as Jewish women have done for centuries on the Sabbath and Hanukkah. It is traditional to sing and tell stories as the candles burn. Let's have your songs.
Woman: Here's a round that's simple to learn.

> *HaNerot halalu anachnu madlikim*
> (We light these candles)
> *Al hanisim v'al hanifla'ot*[15]
> (To remember the miracles and the wonders)
> The women sing the round several times. As they sing the Keeper lights the first candle
> and shuts the room lights.

Let's think of a *kavannah,* our intention in lighting these candles.

> Close your eyes.
> Think of a dark time in your own life.
> What was the light that brought you through this period?
> What inspired you to leave the darkness behind?

The women speak of dark times they have experienced and the light which dispelled those events. Each women tells her story, lighting a candle as she speaks.
Finally, all the candles are lit and the women's sharing is over. We sit, enclosing the light of the *menorot* within our circle, suffused with our warmth.

> We sing together:
> *Banu hoshekh l'garesh,*[16] Hebrew folksong
> This Little Light of Mine, traditional spiritual,
> and back to
> *Ki im Yehudith, bat merari.*

Refreshments:
Food is offered: Salty cheeses—Greek feta, Armenian string cheese, bleu cheese, cheddar and wine—in honor of the miracle Judith wrought.* We also eat foods made with oil—donuts, humus, potato latkes—to commemorate the miracle of the lights.

---

*It is traditional to eat these foods to honor Judith because they were the means by which she slew the enemy, Holofernes. The cheese she fed him made him so thirsty that he gulped down enough wine to fall into a drunken sleep. He thus became an easy target.[17]

TEVET
DECEMBER/JANUARY
A Time To Weep

Bring: Bibles, large decorative box or jar, *Yahrzeit* candles, photos, cakes and wine.

Setting: A living room, at the home of the Keeper of the month. It is in the depth of winter. We sit on pillows and on comfortable chairs. The walls of the room are hung with views of ancient and modern Jerusalem. The room is brightly lit with candles and shaded lamps. Since the theme of *Tevet* evokes sadness and mourning, light is essential for balance. (Dark feelings in a dark room will drain the participants of energy, whereas abundant light will function in dynamic tension with the darkness, enabling energy to flow freely.)

Themes for Tevet
Keeper: *Tevet* is a transitional time in the middle of winter when there are no major holidays. The month's principal event is the Fast of the Tenth of *Tevet*.

On that day, Nebuchadnezzar, the evil King of Babylon, laid siege to Jerusalem, the Holy City. Three years later, after continuous siege, the Temple was destroyed. The tenth of *Tevet* marks the beginning of the Destruction for which we fast on *Tisha B'Av*, the Ninth of *Av*.[1]

During this month we re-experience the destruction of Jerusalem, spiritual center of the Jewish people. Fasting symbolizes our mourning state because the central emblem of our faith, the Holy Temple, has been violated.

It is appropriate at this time to remember the deaths of loved ones, by a *yahrzeit*, the one-year anniversary. I would like to invite all those here who have lost someone within the past year to join with me in marking the transition from formal mourning to gathering our memories of their lives into our own.

Each woman marking a death is given a *yahrzeit* candle.

This is the *yahrzeit* of my grandmother's death, so I shall light a candle for her.[2] (The others light candles.)

Some study Torah together at the *yahrzeit* in honor of the deceased person.[3]

Among the Hasidim the *yahrzeit* is considered to be a time of both sadness and joy. The Hasidim drink and eat, dance and sing, in honor of the dead. I would like to mark the *yahrzeits* of those who have died in this way. This will enable us to experience a ceremony both ancient and modern, like the *Rosh Hodesh* ritual itself. There is a tradition among Jews, one which is prominent throughout the Middle East and other parts of the world, the tradition of women mourners.[4] As the prophet Jeremiah has said:

Thus says the Lord of hosts. Consider, and call for the mourning women, that they may come and send for the wise women, that they may come; and let them make haste, and take up a wailing for us, that our eyes may run down with tears, and our eyelids gush out with waters.[5]

Sign of Tevet

The goat, *G'di,* is the astrological sign of this month. The goat works its way slowly, laboriously up the mountain of winter. Though the path is treacherous, the goat never slips or falls. Sure-footed, firmly centered in the earth, the creature eventually reaches the summit. During *Tevet,* as we focus on the cycle of death and life, we are like that goat, slowly climbing up from the depths of sadness and grief into the light of faith and renewal.[6]

The women share memories about their loved ones who have died, and bring them to life in speech for those present.

Woman: Tell us about your grandmother. What was her name? What memories do you have of her?

Keeper of *Tevet:* My grandmother's name was Sophie which comes from the Greek "Sophia," wisdom. Her Hebrew name was Sarah.

The Keeper shows photos of Sophie, explaining the origin of her grandmother's name. She shows an old jar which once stood on the counter of her grandmother's kitchen.

Keeper: This is a "Memory Jar" in which I keep trinkets, objects and whatever reminds me of my grandmother.[7]

Storytelling:

The Keeper of *Tevet* tells stories and anecdotes about her grandmother. The memories traverse the range of emotions from wistfulness to sadness to happiness to grief and back again.[8] An example follows:

I remember "Granma's" hands. They were always busy doing something, making something. She was stirring the rich brown batter for the honey cake or kneading the soft puffy dough for Sabbath *challot.* She was polishing the stove till it shone like new, or scrubbing dirty footprints off the kitchen floor. Then there were her geraniums which she trimmed, pruned, watered and admired as if they were her children.

In the last years of her life, "Granma" was not able to continue her activities. She had an operation on her hand. The doctor crossed the nerves by mistake, and the loss of use in her right hand left her bereft and helpless. Still, I try to remember all that she used to do.[9]

The Keeper begins to weep and the other women form a circle around her, arms around each other's waists, shoulders.

Group Wailing

Group wailing is inspired by the accounts of the wailing women in Jeremiah and other writings from the ancient Near East.

One woman begins to wail and moan softly in a manner that sounds like a form of blues singing.

"Sometimes I Feel Like A Motherless Child," (spiritual) sung with or without words, is very likely to inspire sadness and grief which is waiting beneath the surface to emerge.

Some follow the voice of the singer, others harmonize. Then, in the magical way in which song is able to open the heart, some begin to weep.

This is a very powerful and moving exercise. However, it is not for everyone. One must not feel obligated to weep. In fact, those who do not feel like weeping can give support and comfort through their physical presence and through the sounds of their voices. The purpose of group wailing is to lend strength in numbers towards the act of unburdening oneself of personal grief. The group provides a safe haven for the individual to weep and mourn, not in isolation as she is accustomed to do in this society, but in a supportive, understanding environment.

In reciprocal fashion, the individual's loss provides the group members with the opportunity to experience grief as well, both for their own personal losses and for that of the Keeper.[10]

Singing

As the wailing ends, the voices of the women revert to song. One woman sings a tune based on the words of the hasid, Rabbi Nachman of Bratzlav, an Eastern European sage and storyteller of the late eighteenth and early nineteenth centuries.

Kol ha-Olam kulo gesher tsar me'od . . . (All the world is a narrow bridge)[11] . . . She sings another tune by a modern Hasidic rabbi, "Return again"[12]

Healing Circle

Woman: As we stand here in the circle, let's focus on the name of the person whose *yahrzeit* is this evening, as well as others we have lost whose names come to mind. As Absalom, the ill-fated son of David knew, it is a sad thing to have no one "to keep my name in remembrance."[13]

We could say these names aloud, inviting the spirits behind the names to come into the circle with us. In this way, we recognize the continuity between life and death, the circle of existence which permeates all being. We agree with Rabbi Simeon who noted in *Pirkei Avot, Sayings of the Fathers,*

There are three crowns: the crown of learning, the crown of priesthood, and the crown of royalty; but the crown of a good name excels them all."[14]

As names come to mind, the women mention them, pausing between each name to let that name have its place within the circle.

Woman: My great aunt Mira, who died this year.

Woman: My friend Nurit who died of cancer this year.

Woman: My father who died ten years ago this month.

Keeper of *Tevet:* I had a dream this month. I know it was about my grandmother even though in the dream her name was Luthi. The story is a message from my grandmother, I think. Until this dream I had not been able to accept her death. I'd like to tell you about it.

My grandmother used to tell this story about a mysterious figure named Luthi, who had migrated to Israel after the Holocaust. She would only say that Luthi was the one who taught people how to grieve after the Holocaust when everyone felt too dead inside to shed another tear.

Storytelling:

LUTHI'S STORY[15]

My grandmother, Sophie, often spoke of the market in Vilna where she had grown up. On Friday mornings just before the Sabbath, one Jew was not afraid to help another. Here in America, she used to say, it's "Every Shopper for Her/Himself and May the Fastest Hands Win!" She told me this story once about how, as a young woman, she met Luthi.

It was shortly after World War II in Cleveland on the day before Pesach. Sophie had gone to the grocery store for some last minute shopping. Aronin's Market was stuffed like a cabbage with people frantically buying for the Holiday of Matzos. In the mélée somebody tugged at her elbow.

"Can you tell me where is the *kosher l'Pesach* cooking oil?" asked a tiny woman with an ancient face, soft and shrivelled like a peach which has lain in the sun too long.

"Nobody helps an old woman," she complained, in the same way my grandmother complained when she could no longer read the recipes she had written down on crackled pieces of paper.

Sophie left her cart and guided the elderly woman by the arm to a bin with only a few bottles of the pristine oil left.

"Thank you," smiled the weathered peach. "This I will remember. You're a good girl."

As my grandmother pushed her cart to the next aisle to find spices, she saw, to her surprise, a small self-contained woman standing in the center of a crowd of curious listeners. People were whispering, as they do when a celebrity is in their midst, "Come, hear Luthi tell stories. That's Luthi. You *must* hear her."

Luthi's face bloomed as she told her stories. Her earrings sparkled, her eyes beckoned, her mouth luxuriated in each well-chosen word. Was this the same woman who, a few minutes earlier, had been too helpless to find oil?

With the whole store listening, she invited every one of those frantic shoppers down, down, down to the hidden world beneath Aronin's Market where the Pesach hubbub did not yet exist, where there were no stores, no shopping lists, no demands on anyone's time.

As she spoke, all found their way down to the basement of the grocery store. At the bottom of the stairs, instead of the expected piles of discarded flour sacks and canned goods, there were more steps. They were covered with grass and were actually part of a graduated playing field. The green color faded by degrees as it sloped downward over the steps. Suddenly, the crowd was outdoors. Spring seemed far behind. Now winter approached slowly, heavy-footed, a dark bear on the prowl.

Luthi stood at the bottom of this green stairway, beckoning. One by one, she called out the names of those present. Where had she learned them? Those who had not yet been called watched the others go down to her silently. Then Sophie was called. She stood face to face with Luthi, her heart drumming inside her chest. In every direction were small holes, no bigger than hands. Each one contained a single flower which stood straight up.

Sophie asked Luthi if she had a sister and Luthi said yes. She asked if Luthi's sister were winter and she were summer, and again Luthi answered yes.

Sophie crouched before an unopened flower and tried to pry it open.

"You mustn't open it," Luthi warned. "It's not ready."

My grandmother examined the flowers more carefully. She knew each one by name. Then she realized that the names that had been called out were the same as the names of the flowers.

Luthi explained, "There is a cycle of people and flowers, their names and growing seasons interchangeable. This garden could have been called Auschwitz or Dachau or Treblinka.

"Each person has a story. That story is the seed from which the flower grows. Tell the story. Bury your pain in the earth like a seed. Your flower will grow."

My grandmother would later say, "No one every explained death that way before. We lost so many of my family back in Vilna, we thought it was bad luck to talk about it; that more death would come of talking about death. But Luthi showed us that from telling the pain, by giving it a name, we could grow new life from our seeds of grief." Sophie was never afraid to talk about death or other subjects most people avoided. Her openness was a gift.

When I awoke from my dream, in that instant I beheld my grandmother's face, and at last I knew with my heart that she had died.

Meditation:[16] Precious Pain

Woman: Now I'd like to meditate. This has helped me in the past in grieving for those people I have lost. As in the story, this meditation will focus on the cycles of life and death. If you want to join me, close your eyes and find a comfortable position. Pay attention to your breathing, in and out, in and out, in and out. . . .

As thoughts come in, just watch them and let them go. All the while keep remembering your breathing, in and out . . . in and out . . . in and out. . . .

Now let your mind come to rest on a person who is no longer in your life, someone whom you loved very much at one time, someone you may still love to this day.

Who was this person? How did you come to know him or her? What brought you together? What caused your lives to intermingle?

Remember how it felt to be with this person. . . .

Now it is time for this person to leave. . . . Allow yourself to experience the pain of that separation. . . . Imagine that your pain is a precious stone which you wrap carefully in material you choose. Take care of your pain. Protect it. Cherish it. Keep it.

This pain is also your memory of the person who you have lost. Find a safe place for this pain and keep it there so you can return to it when you need to.

This pain can also be your teacher. What has your pain taught—about loss, about your relationship with this person, about yourself? Consider what you have learned and hold it inside for a while. . . .

When you're ready, open your eyes.

Keeper of *Tevet:* Let's say Kaddish now. My grandmother used to tell us how much she had wanted to say Kaddish for her father and, of course, she was not allowed to do so. Kaddish is one of my favorite prayers. The words sound like rocking, like a mother rocking a baby—*Yitgadal v'yitkadash shmei rabbo. . . .*[17]

The women recite the prayer affirming the wonder and awe of this universe. All join in the call and respond. Then the Keeper invites the women to read original poetry and prose in the Kaddish mode.

Keeper of *Tevet:* We've come full circle, from grief and mourning to joy and praise, the way our ancestors have always managed to do before us. Let's eat cakes and drink sweet wine now in the Hasidic tradition of *yahrzeit.*

All eat and drink. The *yahrzeit* candles flicker in the darkness in memory of those who have passed away.

S H V A T
JANUARY/FEBRUARY
A Time to Plant

Bring: Fruits of trees: dates, figs, apples, oranges, olives, almonds, bokser (St. John's bread); leafy and/or flowering branches and sprigs, especially an almond branch; flowers; almond cake or cake with one of the above fruits in it; two loaves of whole wheat *hallah;* musical instruments.

Setting: Indoors on a winter evening, in a dining room with a table large enough for the group. We meet this month not on *Rosh Hodesh,* but on the fifteenth of the month, the Full Moon of *Shvat,* on the holiday known as *Tu B'Shvat, the New Year of the Trees.* However, we consider the symbol of the tree in Judaism to have a unique significance for women and so we mark the festival wherever we happen to be.

We wear the colors of Spring and the colors of trees: brown, green, pink, yellow.

The room is filled with the scents of branches, leaves, sprigs, fronds, and fruits we have brought with us. As we enter the house, we place our bouquets around the room.

Themes for Shvat

Keeper: Today we separate one year of growth from another for the purpose of marking certain important years in the lives of trees planted by Jews. *Orlah* is the third year—when one is permitted to prune the tree for the first time. *Shmittah* is the seventh year in the counting of Jewish years—when the earth rests, a Sabbath of the land.

We mark this New Year of the Trees in the middle of Winter, in Shvat. In Israel, there is already a hint of Spring to come.

(She shows a delicate vase of lavender Jerusalem glass containing a white flowering twig.)

This is a branch of the almond tree. It is called *sha-ked,* "watcher," because it is the first tree to blossom each year. It "watches out" for Spring.

Now is the time to hear, feel, and smell the sap starting to thaw and flow again.

By celebrating *Tu B'Shvat* with women only, we'll discover some of the feminine aspects of growth. We have decided to make this Sabbath for women, starting tonight with the *Tu B'Shvat seder* and continuing tomorrow on *Shabbat Shirah,* the Sabbath of Song.[1] Then we'll read in the Torah about the crossing of the Sea of Reeds and chant together *Shirat HaYam,* the Song of the Sea. Tonight our women's seder will be devoted to stories, songs, meditations and foods linking women and trees.

Sign of Shvat

Keeper of *Shvat:* The sign of *Shvat* is *D'li,* the Bucket or Vessel. Woman is a vessel—for fertility, for childbearing, for nurturance and life. In this month, we draw deep into the Well to find what we need to sustain us.

42

Let's think of the Torah as a vessel, pregnant with words, with mean-ings. In Hebrew, the word "Torah" is feminine. The Torah is known as a "Tree of Life."[2] We women are also fruitful trees of life.

Singing: One woman begins and all join in singing *Etz Hayyim Hi* ("She is a Tree of Life" Jewish Liturgy)

Meditation:[3] Etz Hayim: Tree of Life

Woman: Let's meditate on the Tree of Life and imagine the ways of both trees and women.

Find a comfortable position, sitting straight up. Close your eyes and focus on your breathing, inhaling and exhaling. . . .

Imagine your breath as a column travelling from the base of your spine up to your head, and back down the spinal column as you exhale. . . . Imagine your own trunk as that of a living, growing tree. . . . Now at last your sap is beginning to thaw and to flow again . . . feel the sap, the life fluids moving inside you. . . .

A tree is like a woman with vital sap flowing through her: *mayim hayyim,* waters of life, the blood of her period which flows out of her, or which becomes the blood of her child growing in her, the milk filling her breasts, nourishing her infant.

A woman is like a tree reaching for light, breaking through the hard soil, striving for independence, yet recognizing her dependence on all living growth around her.

Torah is a Tree of Life, growing with words, wisdom and meanings. . . .

What kind of tree are you? . . . Do you grow in the desert, on a mountain, in a field, in an orchard? Do birds sing in your branches? Do squirrels climb up your trunk? Do termites gnaw at your wood? How does your bark feel to the touch? What shape are your leaves? What kinds of fruits and flowers do you bear? As a tree . . . as a woman. . . .

Envision the kind of tree you are . . . think of your roots reaching down, down into the earth . . . feel how deep they are. . . . What nourishment do your roots seek in the earth? What nourishment do you seek in the world? What do you need to sustain you? What do you need as a tree? What do you need as a woman?

See your branches and leaves reaching for the light. . . . Feel what it is to be a tree . . what it is to be a woman. . . . (A very full pause) When you're ready, open your eyes.

We return to the circle and share the imaginings experienced in the meditation as they relate to our goals and strivings, our resources and creations as women and as "trees." We discuss the kind of nourishment we are seeking in the world, what we need in order to survive, in order to be fulfilled. We compare what we need as "trees" and as women.

Keeper of *Shvat:* The Tree of Life, *Etz Hayyim,* is an important feminine sym-bol in Judaism. Several women in the Bible have names signifying trees or growing things. Esther in Hebrew is *Hadass,* myrtle. There is *Alon Bachut,* the weeping oak of Genesis 35:8, where Deborah, Rebecca's nurse, died. No one knows why the tree is called *Alon Bachut.* Because I puzzled over the name, I wrote the *midrash* that follows.

Woman: We've arrived at "Nosh 'n Drash," the new all-night coffee house where you can feed body and soul at the same time.[4]

ALON BACHUT, THE WEEPING OAK[5]

In the Garden of Eden one tree drooped sadly when Adam and Eve were expelled. Unlike the other trees who felt that the first human beings deserved punishment for disobeying the command of God, this tree felt only regret. It had been a dwarf for the first years of its life. Other trees had mocked it with teasing names "Stumper," "Flower Face," "Baby Wood." During those years the tree wept continually, the soil becoming so drenched with its tears that nothing could grow near it.

One day it heard a voice from heaven, a *bat kol,* saying, "Do not despair. You have a special purpose. You were placed in the Garden to weep at the death of another tree, an animal, a human being. All that grows and lives must one day die. You will help those who must go on living, listening for the sound of sadness in their hearts, a sound which they cannot utter alone."

Now the tree had a mission: the task of mourning the dead. The tree's tears came when one of its sisters or brothers decayed and fell; when an animal died of starvation; when rain drowned the insects. All were comforted for they were not alone in their grief.

This "tree of lamentation" grew from a small, bent sapling into a sturdy sentinel of the Garden. Winds and birds bore its seed all over the world, carrying the ability to mourn into every garden, field and forest where plants and creatures lived and died.

One of those seeds became the oak under which Deborah, nurse of Rebecca, was buried. The tree mourned long and loud for this beloved member of the family. It came to known as *Alon Bachut,* the Weeping Oak, a bearer of strength in times of need.

About Female Trees:

The story of Tamar comes to mind. Her name means "date palm tree." All we know about her is in Genesis 38.

A bowl of dates is set out in Tamar's honor. One woman recites a blessing, taking a date and displaying it.

Woman: May we know the sweetness in this fruit which comes from the *tamar* and the *adama,* the earth.

All: *Barukh ata Adonai Eloheinu melekh ha'olam borei p'ri ha'etz.* Holy One of Blessing, Your Presence fills creation, forming the fruit of the tree.[6]

If the group wishes, one person may now say the blessing in the feminine.

Woman: *Brukhah at Shekhinah boret p'ri haetz.* Blessed are You, Divine Presence, who has created the fruit of the tree.

One woman tells the story of Tamar in her own words, or reads aloud in Genesis 38 as the others follow. A brief summary of the story follows.

Woman: Tamar is the daughter-in-law of Judah, founder of one of the twelve tribes. She is trying to follow the ancient Israeli laws of levirate marriage. When her husband dies, Tamar marries his younger brother—a custom that will enable her to produce an heir to continue her first husband's name. But when her second husband dies, the suspicious Judah refuses to give his only remaining son to her. He fears that Tamar has caused the deaths of his two other sons. Tamar therefore resorts to disguise and trickery, seducing Judah in order to bear a child. From this offspring will descend the Messiah.

There is a phrase in the text that provides a key to understanding the source of Tamar's strength. This phrase is *petach eynayim* in Genesis 38:14. The literal meaning is "the opening of the eyes." In its Biblical context, it sounds more like a geographic place name which also has a double meaning.

According to the Rabbis, *petach eynayim* may also be viewed as that place within herself where Tamar sought a solution to her plight. Furthermore, the Rabbis considered her to be one of the seven prophetesses, gifted with insight in knowing that she would give birth to an ancestor of the Messiah, which indeed she did.[7]

The tree metaphor may be the clue to the connection between Tamar's story and her name. Like the date tree which bears her name, Tamar had to reach deep down within herself to draw up the sustaining force which would make her fruits grow. As the tree draws up water, Tamar drew up an inner strength that was able to sustain her and that will sustain future generations.[8]

We discuss the questions that come to mind wondering about morality and ethics in the story of Tamar and Judah. We talk about what a woman would have done at other times in Jewish history, and compare this to biblical times. We compare Tamar's story with Ruth's.

Music

A woman leads everyone in singing *"Tzaddik KaTamar Yifrach"* (Righteousness will flourish like a palm tree; Jewish liturgy).

Woman: *Shabbat Shirah,* the "Sabbath of Song" commemorates the Torah portion we read around the time of *Tu B'Shvat;* Exodus 13:17-17. This portion contains the Song of the Sea, sung by Moses and then by Miriam. Remember the midrash which says that the reason Miriam's Song is not given in its entirety is because it is up to each of us to finish the song which she began? Let's try to do this now, accepting Miriam's legacy to us in the form of her Well and her Song. Both symbolize the potential for human creativity and growth which we recognize and celebrate tonight.[9]

We each take simple instruments bells, triangles, sticks, blocks, drums, rattles, etc. One woman begins to sing a *niggun*, the others accompany with their own voices and instruments. Then in the spirit of both *midrashim* and jazz bands, we improvise on the original *niggun*, changing rhythm and mood. We add our own style and our own interpretation to Miriam's song. Eventually, the music winds down.

Eating:

The Keeper invites all to eat the foods of trees after these blessings:

Keeper: May we learn from the almond tree which blossoms fearlessly in the middle of Winter.
All: Amen.

Keeper: *Barukh Ata Adonai Eloheinu Melekh haolam borei minei mezonot.* Holy One of Blessing, Your Presence fills creation, making various kinds of foods.

All: Amen.

A woman sings *HaShkediah Porakhat,* The Almond Tree is Blossoming.
All join in singing and then eat the Almond Moon Dream Cake.

Woman: I made special *hallot* for tonight.[10]

She shows two loaves, one shaped like a pitcher and one shaped like a fish. She first salts the loaves, then takes them in her hands and holds them together.

The pitcher is for the sign of the month, *D'li,* the water-bearer. *Shvat* is the time when life-giving liquids flow through the earth.

The fish is for the Sea of Reeds which we cross together in the Torah portion tomorrow on the Sabbath of Song.

May we learn how to flow in *Shvat,* like the sap in the trees, like the waters in the land, like the fish in the sea. May we learn how to complete Miriam's song in our lifetime, or teach our children how to finish it. May we learn how to let the song that is in us flow out of us.

All: Amen.

Pieces of the warm bread are broken off and passed to each.

Woman: We eat the food before us which represents the seven species of produce in Israel as set forth in Deuteronomy 8:8. These are wheat, barley, vines, figs, pomegranates, olives and honey. Even for those of us who cannot celebrate this agricultural festival in the Holy Land, our connection to the land is thus strengthened by our celebration.

Supplementary Ritual—A Time to Plant:[11]

This ritual may be included as part of the *Tu B'Shvat seder* or performed at another time. The seeds can be planted in flower pots and then transplanted outdoors in the Spring.

Bring: Seed packets of all kinds; soils; flower pots; watering vessel.

Setting: Indoors; a warm place where no one will care if soil spills on the floor.

Leader: I've brought some seeds for us to plant together to mark the New Year of the Trees.

Our sages have designated the fifteenth of *Shvat* as the boundary between one year of growth and another, because the rains of the previous year have already fallen. Any new growth after this day results from the blessings of the New Year.[12] If we plant now, we insure a new supply of blessings for the coming year.

This new planting season is also a metaphor for the seeds of new endeavors taking root in our own lives.

Woman: Let's sing while you're getting the seeds ready. Here's a song from the first line of the first Psalm: *V'haya ka'etz shatul al palgei mayim* (Be like a sapling growing by the streams of water).[13]

(All sing)

Woman: That song reminds me of the idea that "tree" is a metaphor for the just and righteous in the world to come, because the fruits do not appear immediately, but only in future generations, just as in the story in the *Talmud*.

HONI AND THE CAROB TREE[14]

A long time ago, Honi, the Circle-Drawer,* walked in the land of Israel, when he met a man planting a carob tree with his grandchild.

"Old man," chided Honi, "don't you know you'll never live to eat the fruits of this tree?"

"I know that, but my grandchild will. As my grandfather planted for me, so I shall plant for her."

But Honi was not satisfied with this reply, even as he rested on the earth. He slept and slept for many years, and when he awoke he had a long white beard. He was amazed. He saw an old woman picking fruit from a tree nearby to give to a young child with her.

"Is that your fruit tree?" he asked.

"It is mine because my grandfather planted it for me. I tend it so that my grandson can have it also. We have already taken from this tree seeds to plant another one."

It was then Honi remembered what the old man had said to him long ago. He understood that God was giving him a lesson in planting not only for oneself but for generations to come.

The women discuss the story, and give examples in their own lives of providing for future generations. Before they plant, they "find the kavannah" for setting the seeds into the soil. This is done through a guided fantasy in which each person closes her eyes and imagines herself as a specific type of seed. She plants herself wherever she needs new growth: in a new job, new relationship, a new home, a new project. Taking this seed through all the stages of cultivation and growth, she imagines the plant it will become and the fruits and flowers it will bear. When she emerges from her image journey, she opens her eyes.

Keeper: Who wants to plant first? I've brought caraway and fennel and alfalfa and marigold and thyme. There are some mystery seeds, too. Here is soil and water.

The women have opened their eyes, and take turns planting the seeds. As they do this they share "seed fantasies," an opportunity for them to talk about "new seeds" in their lives. Some are learning Hebrew for the first time or a new skill like skiing, weaving, computer programming, chanting Torah; becoming engaged or married; finishing a degree program; or going on a significant journey. Around the circle, each woman shares her seed vision and her *kavannah* for planting.

*So called because of his ability to draw circles in the earth to cause rain.

Woman: I'd like to say a *brachah* for the seed to grow. *Baruch Ata Adonai sh'hagar'in sheli yitzmakh bashemesh u'vachom.* Holy One of Blessing, may my seed grow in the sun and the warmth.

All: Amen.

Singing
Woman: There's a song my mother taught me. She had a beautiful garden in Israel which I helped her tend every summer until she died.

> (She sings *Gar'in katan nattati batelem hashachor* (I put a small seed into the black earth, Hebrew folksong). All join. This recalls to others seed and planting songs: *Hanitsanim nir'u ba'aretz, et hazamir higia* (The buds appear in the land, the time of singing has come, Hebrew folksong); The Garden Song.[15] When each woman has spoken and all have planted their seeds, one woman leads the group in a closing activity.)

Movement
One woman demonstrates a way of moving, taking on the qualities of new seedlings, seed growth underground, seed growth breaking through the earth.

Then as the women each take on the movement characters of their own "seeds," the group as a whole starts to move together as one growing plant or tree.

Alternatively, one woman can be the "gardener," planting seeds and helping them grow by directing and guiding the movements of the women in the group. This method is best for groups which are slow to start moving.

The ritual comes to an end as each woman comes out of her "growing" posture and becomes herself once more.

ADAR ALEPH
FEBRUARY/MARCH
A Time To Be Born

Adar Aleph I: A Pre-Birth/Pregnancy Ritual*

Bring: A cord which has been wrapped around Rachel's Tomb in Israel or, if unavailable, a new cord of a pleasing color. Bring stories and legends of Rachel, the matriarch associated with childbirth.[1] Prepare anecdotes about your own pregnancies and your mother's/grandmothers'/sisters'/aunts' pregnancies.

Keeper: I have brought you this purple cord, Yasmin. A young bride I know wound this very cord around Rachel's Tomb in Israel with a *kavannah* for her fertility and that of other young women who might need Rachel's help. Those who visit Rachel's Tomb in Bethlehem wrap a string around the tomb while praying. This string serves as a reminder of Rachel's prayers, similar to the use of *tefillin,* another example of a string used in the course of prayer. As Rachel died in childbirth, she is thought to be especially compassionate to children in the womb and their mothers, potential and real.

Remembering our foremother, Rachel, is very fitting at the New Moon, for, according to tradition, this is an auspicious time to visit Rachel's burial place. The sacredness of Rachel's Tomb inspires enough *kavannah* for the entire month, and even an entire pregnancy.[2]

Storytelling:

RACHEL'S TOMB

When God was preparing to create the first human being from *adamah,* the earth, the Deity breathed *ruach hayyim,* the spirit of life, into a clod of matter. This became Adam—man.

Then twelve fragments of earth from that first clod settled on the ground to become rocks. It is believed those were the same rocks upon which Isaac was nearly sacrificed on Mount Moriah. A generation later, Jacob found these rocks on his journey from Beer-Sheva to Haran. Addressing the God of his Fathers and Mothers, Jacob said, "If these rocks come together, forming a single large rock, I shall know that I am to become the head of twelve tribes."

Sure enough, the rocks did merge into one. Jacob used this single rock as a pillow for his head while he slept and dreamt of the ladder with angels ascending and descending. (Genesis 27:11-12) It was said later that the same rock was seen at Ephrat on the way to Bethlehem (the location of Rachel's Tomb) and divided itself into twelve rocks once again. That was the place where Rachel, Jacob's wife, gave birth to Benjamin before she died. This was after she had experienced twelve years of infertility and after she had fasted for twelve days so that she would conceive.

*This ritual is appropriate when a mother-to-be first announces her pregnancy to the community of women, and may be included in any of the months chosen or used separate from *Rosh Hodesh* rituals at a time designated. Here, the expectant mother is called Yasmin.

The eleven grown sons of Jacob then arranged eleven stones at the place where they buried Rachel. Jacob added the final rock, thus making twelve. This was how *Kever Rachel*, the Tomb of Rachel, was built.

Let's now focus on Yasmin and the child in her womb. The matriarch, Rachel will be our guide.
All are silent for a time, concentrating on Yasmin and her baby and Rachel, the compassionate mother.

Keeper: Now, as we think about Yasmin and Rachel, we each take hold of a section of the cord. Let's form a circle with it around Yasmin.
The women stand, surrounding Yasmin with the cord and their positive thoughts for her wellbeing. After a silence of several minutes, the Keeper gives the cord to Yasmin, telling her that if she wishes she can wear it, especially when she feels the need for Rachel's presence.

Keeper: Despite the advances of medical science and technology, pregnancy and birth are times of great danger for mother and child. The folk traditions of Judaism are full of practices designed to protect them.[3]
At this time, the group may choose to present the expectant mother with a special work of calligraphy or an amulet designed to protect a pregnant woman, to inspire and sustain her throughout the coming weeks and months.[4]

Yasmin: Thank you all for your strength and your *kavannot*.
A *niggun* is sung; soon, one by one, the women leave the circle.

Adar Aleph* II—A Ritual of Birth**

Bring: A large bowl with water, facecloths, towels, perfumes and oils, photos of the new family. Women are asked to prepare a song, poem, story, ritual object or special refreshment for the new mother and child. Flowers and fruit are brought for decoration.

Setting: An evening in late winter. We are gathered in the living room of Yasmin who became a new mother last month.[5] The room is decorated with gaily-colored flowers and fruits brought by the women. Photos of the new mother as a baby, the new mother with her mother, and the new mother and

---

*The Hebrew letters also stand for numbers, i.e., *Aleph* is 1, *Beth* is 2, *Gimel* is 3, etc. See *Themes of the Month,* for an explanation of the two *Adars.*
**Usually at the celebration of a life-cycle event that occurs at a *Rosh Hodesh* such as this, friends and relatives who do not usually attend are invited. Every effort is made to welcome them into the group.

father with their new daughter are displayed. The new mother has painted designs with the ten *sefirot,* mystical attributes of God, and placed them around the room.[6] One of these attributes also happens to be the name of the new baby.

Themes for Adar Aleph and Beth

Keeper: This is the *Rosh Hodesh* of *Adar Aleph, Adar* 1. *Adar Aleph* falls between *Shvat* and *Adar Beth, Adar* 2. The extra *Adar* is a necessary adjustment in the Jewish calendar due to the lunar reckoning of the months within a solar year. For example, to avoid having Hanukkah, the Festival of Lights, occur in midsummer, an extra month must be added during specific years of a cycle designated 19 year cycle. These are the 3rd, 6th, 8th, 11th, 14th, 17th, and 19th years.[7]

Since Haman's wicked decree to do away with the Jews was made in a leap year during the second *Adar,* we celebrate Purim at that time. There is another reason why Purim occurs during *Adar.* The redemptions of Queen Esther and Moses occur in sequence.[8]

For *Rosh Hodesh* of the first *Adar,* we celebrate a birth. For *Rosh Hodesh* of the second *Adar,* we look toward the festival of Purim.

Tonight we celebrate a *Yoledet,* a party for the mother of the newborn. If the child is adopted and not necessarily a newborn, we also mark its entry into the mother's life this way. The *Yoledet* is a tradition among the Jews of Yemen which inspired us, as it was just what Yasmin needed one month after becoming a mother.[9]

This *Rosh Hodesh* seemed to be a good time for a ritual exclusively for mother and child and women friends. The baby-naming ceremony takes place before the whole community, as it is the rite of passage during which the child formally enters the Jewish fold. So we welcome Tiferet, Yasmin's new baby, into the Jewish women's community, which includes our ancestors Eve, Lilith, and the Matriarchs!

Woman: It is significant to mark the *Yoledet* now, when we have ended *Shvat,* the month of planting trees. We look forward toward *Adar* with its festival of Purim, and then to *Nisan,* which marks our emergence as a Jewish people.

Now is the crossroad of Winter and Spring, when the earth starts to give birth to the earliest buds, like the almond blossom. To me this season means a coming out, finding what is most essential inside the earth, inside myself. This presages the fastidious cleaning we do before Pesach. It makes us remember what a child's birth means: making room for what is most essential—the raw continuity of life.

Sign of the Month: *Dagim,* two fish. See *Adar Beth,* the next chapter.

Introductions
Keeper of Adar Aleph: Yasmin, introduce us to your friends.

Yasmin: I've invited two of my oldest and dearest friends to celebrate with us tonight. This is Shoshanna and here is Daphne. (She also introduces the "regulars.") And, this is Tiferet who was just four weeks old two days ago.

Woman: Let's sing lullabies to Tiferet and Yasmin as a way of finding our *kavannah* for this evening's ritual. (Spontaneously, the women sing lullabies, weaving a peaceful mood around the room.)
Lyla, lyla;[10] *Shlof, mayn kind;*[11] *Numi, numi;*[12] *Unter Tiferet's (Sarale's) vigele (Traditional); Kumbaya (African);* The Mockingbird Song (Traditional); Pretty Horses (Black Slave lullaby).

Keeper of Adar Aleph: I'd like to explain how the idea for tonight's ritual developed.

About six weeks after each of my children were born, my deepest wish was to bring together my women friends and share my baby. I felt that way especially when my daughter was born. But it never happened. Six weeks after the baby is born, you don't feel like doing it all yourself. There's too much else to do.

Then I heard about the *Yoledet,* where after a woman has a baby, the entire community comes together. They gather in and around her bedroom to celebrate with her and the baby, by singing and feasting. I thought it would be wonderful to do this for Yasmin and her daughter, Tiferet.

I've brought bowls for a *mikveh,* perfumes and oils (shows the bowl of scented water). Some images that came to me when I prepared for today were water, roundness and red roses. Water derives from birth fluid in the womb; waters of creation and purification. Roundness comes from the shape of the pregnant woman and that of the child within her, and the shape of a circle of life and death. For me, red roses represent the lips of the vagina and the interior chambers of the womb. Red roses also imply an unfolding.

Yasmin: I brought these. (She shows an afghan with a blue, pink and yellow diamond pattern.) My grandmother made this, and gave it to me before her death. At that time she began making things for all her granddaughters' children, even those unborn. I was the first grandchild and she prepared this for my firstborn (shows an old tallit). This belonged to my grandfather, given me when he died. Tiferet will be given this when she becomes bat mitzvah.
(Points out photos in the room.) This is my baby picture, and this is my mother's. Here is a picture of me and my mother at my own bat mitzvah.

Studying Torah:
Keeper of *Adar Aleph:* Let's study some texts from the Talmud and the *Midrash* that mention birth. We will see how the rabbis approached conception, pregnancy and birth.*

Yasmin presents an anecdote about her newborn's name—Tiferet.

---

*Distribute copies as per Addenda, Adar Aleph. Each group chooses texts of interest to them and examines them for discussion as per suggested questions.

THE NAME

Her name struck me during a meditation on the *sefirot* which I did as part of the pre-birth *kavannot*.[13] In readying myself for birth, I concentrated on an image I received of the ten *sefirot*, ten different attributes or emanations of God. Each emanation corresponds to a part of the body. The third emanation, from the heart, is *tiferet*. The two emanations surrounding *tiferet* are *gevurah—strength, the left arm; and hesed*—kindness, the right arm.[14]

Each emanation is also related to a certain figure in the Bible. *Tiferet* is Jacob struggling with the angel in the desert. *Hesed* is the famous hospitality of Abraham. *Gevurah* is the fortitude of Isaac who was nearly sacrificed.

Now, of course, there are female equivalents of each of the *sefirot*. For example, *gevurah* is also the heroism of Judith. *Hesed* is the kindness of Ruth whose story parallels Abraham's in many ways.[15] *Tiferet* is Rachel weeping for her children.

My mother passed away three years ago and her Yiddish name was Faige, which means "bird." In English she was Frances. But I just couldn't name my daughter Frances. It felt too close, even though there is the tradition of naming a child after a dead relative.

So, I took the "f" and "r" from Frances. These became the *peh* and *resh* of Tiferet. Then her middle name, Sassona, occurred to me. I like its meaning of "joy, delight," so the last four letters of "Frances" became the *sin, sin,* and *nun* of Sassona.[16]

Woman: And now your mother will always be there in the name of your daughter.

Mikveh:

Keeper of *Adar Aleph:* (To Yasmin) Now we would like to bathe and massage you.

Yasmin is pleased. She goes to a mat placed on the floor. Yasmin lies down comfortably. The Keeper lights candles around the room, shuts off the electric lights, brings out the perfumed water, oils and several face cloths. Those who wish to may take a cloth, dip it into the warm water and bathe Yasmin's face, neck, arms, hands, legs and feet. This activity is an especially healing one for a new mother who has had to become caretaker for a tiny, helpless baby overnight. For this brief time, the new mother can feel as if she is being cared for by many mothers. This is the purpose of the *Yoledet*.

Singing:

As the women "bathe" the new mother, they sing from *Song of Songs* and from the Sabbath liturgy, especially songs which contain the name of the newborn child:

Lekha Dodi - Come my beloved (Sabbath liturgy); *Yasis Elayikh*

Elohayikh - Your God will make you joyful (traditional);

Ani l'Dodi[17] - I am my beloved's; *Kol Dodi Hineh Zeh Ba* - Here comes the voice of my beloved (traditional); *Iti m'Levanon* - With me, from Lebanon (traditional).

The women sing to mother and child while the child sleeps.

Now those who have brought original poems or songs offer them. Then we are ready for an introspective exercise.

Meditation: The Child Within[18]

We meditate beginning with a *niggun*. One woman sings a simple melody, repeating *la, la, la* . . . She leads the group.

Woman: Now, as you are singing, listen to how the melody moves through your body. Sing the same tune for about ten minutes, feeling your energy rise and fall at different points in the process. Never let go of the melody, even when you become tired. . . . Feel the effect in your body and head. . . . Take a moment and breathe in the stillness around you . . . know this stillness as the *shalom* within . . . shalommmmmmm . . . feel its reverberation. . . . When you sing this way, the music flows through you like a purifying stream, regenerating your will and your energy.

Now you are ready to meditate on The Child Within.

Take a step inside—follow a guide to the center of yourself.

Close your eyes and breathe in the air around you, the source of your energy.

Listen to the gentle rise and fall of your breath.

Imagine a moment in this quiet where you felt strongly at one with the earth that surrounded you, where you were rooted in the universe.

Perhaps it was when you were a child. . . . Remember that time. . . . Connect yourself with this innocent wonder-filled child within . . . take her to you. . . . Imagine taking her by the hand and following her to a place where she leads you. . . . She is your creation of your younger self, full of light and hope. . . .

Now, in any way you need to, ask her to stand with you, to become your best teacher on this journey. . . . Imagine her beaming at you, shining with light . . . she is aglow, and when you touch her, you feel her energy envelop you. . . . Stand together, bathed in the warm light, and reach out to embrace her. Take her into your arms, into yourself. . . . She is yours to keep, *she is you*. . . .

Now move back from that awareness into the spirit of your present life.

Introduce your child, your guide into that space.

Promise her that you will call on her for help when darkness clouds your vision. Make a promise. This can be a *kavannah*, a direction for you.

Be still . . . be with the light . . . listen once again to your breath . . . to the sounds that surround you.

Return to an awareness of your body, of the room around you. . . .

You have strengthened yourself by joining with yourself.

When you open your eyes, share this journey with others if you feel so moved.

(Some of the women share the details of their "journeys.")

Gifts for the Child:

Woman: I'd like to give Tiferet something I learned in my meditation. Tiferet, may you know the strength and joy of being female.

Woman: Tiferet, may you join in the continuity of the cycles of the moon, may you turn gracefully with the cycles of your own life.

Woman: Tiferet, may you receive sustenance and comfort from the earth.

Woman: Tiferet, I give you the love of all here.

Woman: I give you the wisdom and the will to listen to your own heart.

Keeper of *Adar Aleph:* (whispering) Tiferet, Tiferet, Tiferet, Tiferet . . .

(All join in whispering around her head and body, reinforcing the power of her own name.)

Woman: Yasmin, I'd like to share an insight I had when my daughter was born thirteen years ago, one that is still with me today.

This is the idea of separation, of *havdalah,* going all the way back to the very beginning when the land and the water were first separated. The land came out of the water, and that was a good separation, in the words of the Creator.[19]

I felt that way when my daughter was born—just seeing her head when she was still coming out of me.

In the context of Shabbat, we usher in *Shabbat HaMalkah,* the Sabbath Queen, with a blessing over wine. At the end of Shabbat we say *Havdalah,* and again bless the wine. There needs to be a separation, but there is hope that it will be a good separation, that some of what we have gained during *Shabbat* will stay with us.

At this time I've finished breastfeeding my daughter, but she's still dependent on me for her food. Yet, as I watch, she grows more able to do things alone, to work things out by herself.

And so, my blessing for both of you, Yasmin and Tiferet, is that as you grow, as the separation continues, it should be a good separation. The bond should keep changing while growing stronger.[20]

Yasmin and others: Amen.

Singing:

The women take up the *niggun* which began the meditation, singing softly. Now that Tiferet has awakened, she is passed around to the others. All take turns holding her. As Tiferet makes happy sounds, food is presented: hard boiled eggs in an egg salad, lentils, chickpeas, round moon cookies, two round *hallot* and sweet wine. The round foods are eaten as a way of ingesting the secret of the life cycle.

As the *Yoledet* comes to a close, Tiferet has become a link to the community of Jewish women, past, present and future. Yasmin's new status as a mother has been recognized and affirmed. She has been welcomed back into the community after leaving it to participate in the transitional world of giving birth.

—— RITUALS IN PROGRESS ——

Photos by Ilene Perlman

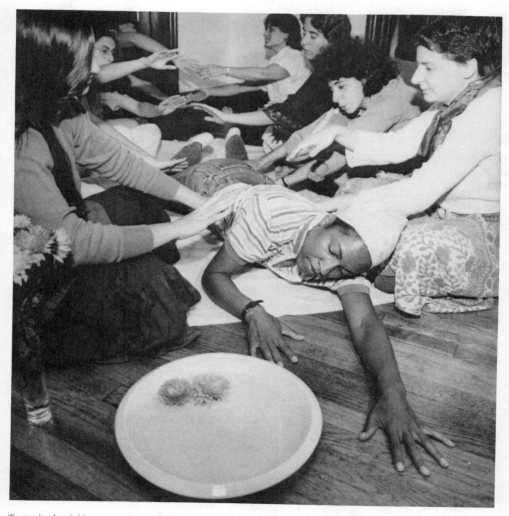

(Some ritual activities occur in more than one month)

Yetsiat Mitzrayim: Coming out of Egypt—
A *mikveh* of song. (Nisan)

Dancing and singing with the bride-to-be
(Elul)

Comforting the woman in mourning (Tevet/Tammuz)

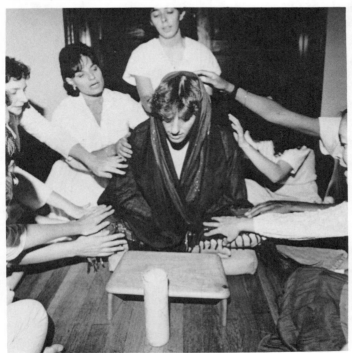

Women in these photos are:
Penina V. Adelman, Matia Angelou,
Miriam Bronstein, Betsy Cohen,
Benji Jackson, Reena Kling,
Elana Klugman, Elyse Landesberg,
Stephanie Loo Ritari.

Making the sign of "Shma" at the *Bagrut*,
Coming of Age ritual (Sivan)

Celebrating the big *Rosh Hodesh—Rosh
HaShanah* (Tishre)

Making masks for Purim (Adar Bet)

Planting the Tree of Life (Shvat)

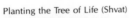

The "Kapparot Ceremony", performed before
the Day of Atonement, as seen in a woodcut
dating back to Augsburg, 1530

סעודת הברית סנדק ווימ

Feast at Childbirth

ADAR BETH
FEBRUARY/MARCH
A Time to Hide;
A Time to Reveal

Bring: Paper bags, crayons, colored paper, scissors, glue and other materials for making masks. Refreshments are customary.

Setting: Evening of the new moon of *Adar.** In keeping with the playful tone of the month, we place our *Rosh Hodesh* festival in a mythical time and place. The room can be set to resemble a Persian women's court of long ago, with small oriental rugs and large floor pillows. Prints of ancient Persia can be hung, showing colored tiles and pleasure gardens, etc. The women have been asked to dress in pajamas or loose slacks, and silk, velvet or fine embroidered blouses, suggesting women of Queen Esther's court.

Themes for Adar Beth

Secretiveness and revelation are central. Queen Esther embodies this theme in her actions when she reveals she is a Jew in order to save her people. Even her name—Esther, "she who is hidden," emphasized this.

In the Purim festival, we re-enact the Esther story through reading and humorous playacting in the synagogue. In this *Purimshpiel,* we hide our identity in costume and role reversal. A special *mitzvah* of Purim is for both sexes to reverse dress and behavior.

It is traditional to improvise skits for enjoyment and entertainment on this theme. The beautiful and wise Esther changes place with the wicked and angry Vashti. Esther turns the tables on Haman. The season also repeats the theme. Winter and its dying vegetation give way to Spring and greenery.

Sign of the Month

Dagim—two fish swimming in opposite directions, like mirror images. Vashti and Esther are like these two, trading places in the court of Ahasuerus, projecting opposite personalities. Vashti is bold, impetuous, haughty. Esther is wily, reserved, seductive.

Queen Esther was also an important figure of hope and redemption for the Marranos who were forced to convert to Christianity during the Spanish Inquisition (1492-1765). Later many practiced Judaism in secret.

We read together a Marrano tribute to Esther.[2]

Storytelling

ESTHER AND VASHTI

Esther and Vashti, the two famous wives of King Ahasuerus, continue *Adar's* theme of dynamic opposites. The story in *Megillat Esther* describes how King Ahasuerus commanded his

*The group should have read the story of Purim as preparation.[1]

56

beautiful wife, Vashti, to appear before a party of drunken ministers to entertain them. When she refused, he banished her from his kingdom and sought a new wife who would be more compliant to his wishes. He chose Esther who was able to gain his confidence and trust, and who later was able to save her people.

The two women represent stages of woman's consciousness. The first stage, symbolized by Vashti, is one of resistance and suggests the initial period of the women's movement in recent years. In it, women realize their oppression in the context of a strict patriarchal society. Compromise is not an option. This stage is characterized by women's struggle to achieve an enduring sense of self-worth. She resists any action that might belittle her.

The second stage, symbolized by Esther, is one of political strategy. More secure in her societal position, she feels free to bend in the direction of long-range goals. In the Purim story, Esther possesses an enlarged vision which enables her to devise a way to combat the oppression of women in Persian society which included Jews as well.[3]

Vashti may mean "beauty" in Persian. Some interpretations suggest that the reason she refused to appear before her husband, Ahasuerus, and his ministers had nothing to do with modesty or high morals. She was ashamed to be seen naked because God had afflicted her with leprosy. Some legends infer that she had grown a tail and that this was why she declined to show herself.

According to the commentaries, Vashti and Lilith could be distant cousins. Each refused to comply with a husband's request. For this, each was banished and her name became associated with evil, blasphemy, and outspokenness.[4]

According to the *Midrash*, Esther is like the moon who brought light to Israel at a time of its greatest darkness. As in the *Scroll of Esther*, "The Jews had light and gladness, and joy and honor,"[5] for Esther delivered the Jews from the hands of Haman. Esther is a symbol of the Jewish people, for, like the moon, they too have waned and waxed throughout history as they survive persecution.

Esther's name itself connects her to the moon. The Hebrew root of her name, *samekh-tav-resh*, means "to hide." Like the moon, Esther was able to keep her identity a secret until the right moment. When the Jews were in dire need, she revealed that she was a Jew and that Haman was about to destroy her people. She shone her light onto the darkest evil and effaced it.[6]

Esther has also been linked to Ishtar and Astarte, goddesses of the ancient Near East. Her name bears a relation to theirs, indicating that her story may be a later version of a myth of a goddess of love and beauty. She is referred to as *"ayyelet ha-shachar,"* the morning star, Venus. Tradition has it that Esther recited Psalm 22 during her three days of fasting. The psalm begins, "To the music-keeper at the time of the morning star," when she retired to her private place in the palace, and with her women, fasted and prayed for three days in order to dispel Haman's evil decree to execute the Jews.

Now that the background for the female characters of Purim has been set, the Keeper of *Adar Beth* explains what the special focus of this *Rosh Hodesh* is to be.

Ta'anit Esther, Fast of Esther

Keeper: Tonight, as part of our celebration of the month of *Adar Beth,* we'll go back in history to the days preceding the first Purim.

At this time Queen Esther refrained from all food and drink and did not see her husband. She did so in order to purify herself before exposing Haman's dire plot to destroy the Jews. As she says to her uncle, Mordecai,

> Go, gather together all the Jews who are present in Shushan, and fast for me, and neither eat nor drink for three days, night and day: I also and my maidens will fast likewise, and so I will go in to the king, though it is against the law: and if I perish, I perish.[7]

Tonight, each of us is a member of Queen Esther's court. She and her maidens probably passed those days of fasting with prayer, song and story. That is how we shall pass the time tonight.

Discussion:

We discuss Esther's fast, focusing on these points: How did separation from her husband help fulfill her mission? How did refusing nourishment strengthen her spiritually so that she could foil Haman's plot and save her people.

We talk about the story of Purim, its meaning for us, and how it may have changed over the years.

Purimshpiel (Purim Play):[8]

We decide to act out some of the attributes of *Adar Beth* and the *Purim* story. One woman suggests we first meditate to stimulate our creative juices and then make masks.

Meditation: Turning Over the Earth

Woman: This is a meditation which will deepen our understanding of the essence of *Adar Beth*, and facilitate role-playing.

Find a comfortable sitting position and become aware of your breathing.

Take several very deep breaths in and out . . . (Repeat). . . . As thoughts and distractions enter, don't fight them. Just watch them and let them go by. . . . Close your eyes . . . and keep breathing in and out. . . . (Repeat)

We are now in the month of *Adar.* The time of turning the soil; giving it a chance to rest, to recover its lost nutrients, to renew itself. We bring up from the earth the deeper, richer unused soil with any tool at hand. Keep turning the soil. . . .

Adar is a turning point of the year, Winter turns to Spring, death turns to life, old turns to new.

Put down your digging tool and think of Esther's story, of Vashti and Esther, or Mordecai, Haman, and Ahasuerus . . . Now, as if you were choosing a Purim mask for yourself, become one of them . . . Take on the personality, looks, bearing, gestures, and voice of this person . . . What do you have to change in yourself to become him or her? How do you feel as this person? Sit with these feelings for a while. . . . (Silence for several minutes)

What insight have you gained from becoming this person who resides beneath the layers of your personality in rich, fertile soil?

What have you learned from turning over the soil, renewing your own earth? (Silence for at least five or ten minutes.)

When you are ready, open your eyes and return to us, here at our *Rosh Hodesh,* to your place in our circle.

Mask-Making:

Woman: With those images still fresh in mind, let's make masks. Then we'll be set for our *Purimshpiel.* (She places paper bags, colored paper, glue, scissors, crayons, etc., in the center of the circle. She helps all the women create masks to wear tonight.)

The mask may be inspired from your meditation and reveal a face you yourself never exhibit or one you are eager to reveal—whatever kind of mask you want to make.

(We work sometimes with serious intent, sometimes singing)
Songs for Mask-Making:
1. *Achen ata El Mistater* (traditional, Hasidic)
   You are a Hidden God (apt for the word-play with Esther, hidden)
2. *LaYehudim hayeta ora v'simcha sasson vikar*
   The Jews had light and joy and gladness and honor
   Ken tiheyeh lanu
   So may it be for us (*Book of Esther* 8:16)
3. *Mi sh'nichnas Adar marbeh b'simcha* (Talmudic folksong)
   Whoever enters Adar increases joy

When we finish making masks, we wear them. There is laughter followed by gasps of surprise and wonder. Still wearing masks, we re-introduce ourselves, explaining who we have become. We share the reasons for our choices.[9]

We are led to a discussion of beauty and artifice as these concepts relate to the ·actions of Vashti and Esther and to our own perceptions of ourselves as women. We consider these questions: What is your notion of beauty? How did it begin? Has it changed since you were a child, teenager, young woman? What is your attitude towards make-up? Your mother's attitude? Your grandmother's attitude?

Purimshpiel:

We decide to act out our ideas on the themes of *Adar Beth*. Forming groups of three to five people, we use questions, the answers to which will become skits or scenes.[10]

After we have performed our *Purimshpiel,* we "break our fast" and eat a light meal or buffet together.

NISAN
MARCH/APRIL
A Time To Rejoice

This month has three names. The first is *Hodesh HaRishon,* the first month, so called to mark the time we became a people. The Jewish New Year, Rosh HaShanah, in *Tishre,* marks the creation of the world. According to the Jewish way of reckoning time, each month represents a distinct beginning; hence, *Hodesh HaRishon* is *Nisan's* historical appellation. The month is also called *Hodesh He'Aviv,* the month of Spring. Finally, the month is named *Nisan,* which may be related to *nitzan,* bud. As King Solomon wrote in the Song of Songs, *"HaNitzanim nir'u ba'aretz* (The buds appear in the land)/*Et hazamir higi'a* (The time of singing has come)."[1]

Bring: Musical instruments: bells, drums, flutes, whistles, tambourines, sticks, scrapers, rattles, kitchen pots; large bowl of water; writing paper; empty coffee can; and matches.

Setting: By the sea or a body of fresh water to remind us that the womb is like a sea through which each of us has passed at the moment of birth. Water also reminds us of the Sea of Reeds through which we, the Jewish people, have emerged to become a nation.

If it is not possible or convenient to meet at a watering place, decorate the space with symbols of Egypt and slavery; liberation, Spring, and the sea. Create a warm environment for Miriam and her community of Jewish women.

Themes for Nisan
Keeper: On *Rosh Hodesh Nisan* we honor Miriam *HaNevia,* Miriam the Prophetess, who died on this day.[2] We call this *Ilui Miriam,* the Exaltation of Miriam.

The focus of this *Rosh Hodesh* will be on our ancestor, Miriam. As a prophetess who could see deeply into the present to understand the future, she also cared for her family, showing heroism. She was not only a poet, a leader of song and dance, but also a midwife.

Woman: We honor Miriam with music, singing and dancing. We honor her with stories; we honor her with poetry.

Keeper of *Nisan:* As we gather on this *Rosh Hodesh,* we imagine ourselves as descendants of that community of women who accompanied Miriam with song and dance to celebrate the safe crossing of the Sea of Reeds—the successful flight from Egyptian slavery. The *Zohar* teaches that we were all present at Mt. Sinai. The mystics and those with deep imagination can uniquely recollect this.[3]

On the 14th of *Nisan* we celebrate the festival of Pesach, the birth of the Jewish people. The grass of *Nisan* is pulsing with the same green that drove our ancestors to procreate.

Sign of the Month

Taleh, the Ram, is the male sheep thrusting into Spring. *Nisan* embodies the fiery urge to create and to procreate; to begin.

Two brothers and a sister assisted at the birth of the Jewish people. Moses is the Ram who knows how to make his way through the unmarked desert. The others follow him. Aaron is the priest who tries to coax the sacred from a calf-shaped golden mound, reassuring those who have lost hope. Miriam leads the song and dance. She teaches the sounds which the sea has taught her, in a chorus of voices—the exultant tenor of the wind, the chiming bell of the sky, the bellowing bass of the mountains, the mournful croak of the valleys, the newfound voice of the people.

> And Miriam the prophetess, the sister of Aaron, took a timbrel in her hand; and all the women went out after her with timbrels and dances. And Miriam answered them, Sing to the Lord, for he has triumphed gloriously; the horse and his rider has he thrown into the sea.[4]

Now, one woman tells a brief version of the Exodus story or else reads the story from the Bible.

Woman: Let's join hands in a circle for a few moments. We will feel the presence of Miriam and her women. Let's each think of our own *kavannah,* our goal for this *Rosh Hodesh Nisan.*

> Silence for several minutes as the women join hands, sitting in a circle with eyes closed, focusing inward. Some of the women share their *kavannot.* An example follows:

Woman: During this month our ancestors had to leave possessions behind and move on to a new way of life. When we leave a place or when we end a portion of our lives and move to something new, how many times do we leave it the way we'd really like to? How many times do we have a closing that really feels more like a renewal and not an ending, a forgetting or an escape? We need to find ways to focus on ourselves in the midst of change and movement. There is always a center within us.

Keeper of *Nisan:* I shall ask Four Questions on this *Rosh Hodesh Nisan* in the tradition of the Four Questions of the Pesach Haggadah.

> —How can we leave *Mitzrayim* (Egypt) behind us?
> —In what ways is the festival of *Pesach* a birth?
> —Why is Miriam's Song unfinished?
> —Why do we say, "By the merit of righteous women we came out of Egypt?"[5]

Purification Ritual/Burning Mitzrayim:[6]

Woman: I propose a Purification Ritual which is an answer to "How can we leave *Mitzrayim* behind?" The Hasidim believe that everyone can be said to be in an individual *Mitzrayim* from which it is crucial to be extricated. This ritual will help us remove the barriers that block celebrating Pesach and experience the life-giving spirit of Miriam.

Let's begin by believing we're in Egypt, *Mitzrayim. Mitzrayim* means "from the straits, the narrows." This is the place where we were slaves, constricted and confined.

Think of what you would like to leave behind this month as you emerge from slave to free person, from seed to blossoming flower, from Winter to Spring.

Take a piece of paper and a pencil (now placed in the middle of the circle). Make a list of qualities, attitudes, fears, and anxieties that are constraining you. The act of writing your *Mitzrayim* is not an act of liberation in itself. This is merely one step in the process. By writing and then burning your *Mitzrayim,* you will be identifying what deters you. Then you need to try to obliterate these negative aspects of your life.

Each woman takes a piece of paper and pencil and writes for about ten minutes.

Woman: (Shows an empty coffee can and matches placed on a fireproof surface) Who would like to begin?
Woman: I shall.

She tears her page of *Mitzrayim* into tiny pieces, dropping them into the can, then lights a match and also drops it in. The others follow suit, some with nervous laughter, some with grins and some with relieved sighs. When the small fire is extinguished, the women who has led the ritual takes the coffee can and turns it upside down, scattering the *Mitzrayim* to the winds. If the gathering is indoors, the ashes should obviously be deposited out of a window or porch.

Woman: We leave our *Mitzrayim* by becoming aware of what constricts us. We also leave behind the "narrow straits" by doing what brings us joy—singing and dancing and telling stories.

Singing:
One woman hums a *niggun,* others follow. Instruments are given. Soon a rhythm is established, punctuated by drums and tambourine. The music grows louder and softer, faster and slower—like the ever-changing sea embracing the shore and receding from it.

Gradually the music fades and conscious, voiced rhythmic breathing follows, imitating the sound of the sea. Then silence.

Chanting:
Woman: Let's chant together a page from the *Haggadah of the Thirteen Sisters,*[7] the beginning of an answer to "How is the festival of Pesach like a birth?"

All chant in unison

Our liberation comes from inside
From *Tehom* the motherdeep, the birthplace inside each of us
From twisted stomachs
From holding it in and making it tight:
Tight womb, tight vagina, tight mouth pressed in upon itself;

Our liberation has been a slow birth over centuries.
Avadim Hayinu, we have been slaves
To words, to prayers, to rituals that do not come from inside,
From *Mitzrayim,* from the desperate push to be whole women,
Whole human beings;

Our liberation will need the old ways of listening to our bodies
To hear the rhythms of the universe reflected therein:
The ocean waves coming close and going away,
The moon herself filling up and emptying out,
The breath gaining and sighing,
The womb blood surging and gushing out,
The womb herself lying fallow for a time and fertile for a time;

Our liberation.
Can you feel how it will be to hear through this inner ear again?
To stop being afraid to be women
Who give birth in the fields,
Who suckle and nurture ideas as we nurture and suckle children,
Who feed ourselves and others from kitchens that are cornucopias,
Who pray like Hannah and Sarah and Eve and our great-grandmothers
And grandmothers who drew from the Well and always found water,
Who pass on wisdom as our mothers passed to us in their milk
The pain-and-joy puzzle in being women.

Our liberation will not be *our* liberation until we share it,
Teach it, feed it, drink it, sign it with the others.
A diamond cannot show *all* its facets until another diamond grinds it.
This is certain: the soft-strong humming waters of *mikveh*
In which we bathe each month
Ache to be born in all of humankind.

Storytelling

Woman: Pesach teaches us about birth, both physical and spiritual. The stories of Miriam abound with themes of creativity, birth, and redemption: the Legend of Miriam's Well weaves these together.

THE LEGEND OF MIRIAM'S WELL

At twilight on the second day of Creation, God embedded a precious liquid jewel in the earth, a miraculous well of pure, sparkling water. From one generation to the next, the well belonged to those who knew how to draw up its water. Filled with *mayim chayyim,* living waters, the well was a reminder to all who drank or drew from it, that Torah, the way of the Jewish people, is also a well from which all may drink and be restored.[8]

Possession of the well passed from Abraham, the first patriarch,[9] to his concubine, Hagar,[10] and then to his son, Isaac.[11] Each of the patriarchs and matriarchs in turn discovered anew this source of living water in the desert.[12]

During their Egyptian slavery, the Children of Israel lost access to the well itself. Worse, they lost the memory that such waters had ever existed.

Only by the merit of Miriam, sister of Moses and Aaron, did the well reappear to them during their desert wanderings. But why was the well revealed in the name of Miriam?

The power of her voice and her intimate understanding of water were the reasons she was thought worthy to be the keeper of the well.

She convinced her father, Amram, to restore conjugal relations with her mother, Yocheved, because in a dream she learned that a liberator of Israel would be conceived from their union.[13] Later she sang to the Nile River, persuading it to protect her baby brother, Moses. She had placed him in the reeds close to the banks to save him from Pharaoh's evil decree that all Jewish baby boys should be destroyed at birth.

As a midwife in Egypt she had also used her voice in her work. Known by the name Puah, which means "breath," she used to puff gentle sounds and songs into the ears of a woman about to give birth. With a voice calming as the rippling of water, Miriam coaxed reluctant newborns out of the womb and into the world.[14]

After the Israelites had crossed the Red Sea, Miriam and the women took up instruments as they danced and sang the song of redemption.[15] Once again, Miriam's reverence for water inspired her to lead a joyful song of salvation. Thus was Miriam's unique connection with the sources of redemption begun both in Egypt and in the desert exile of her people.[16] It was believed then that God gave the well in Miriam's name, since Moses could barely speak, let alone sing, while the voice of Aaron, the priest, was so loud that it frightened both children and animals.

Later, when Miriam passed from the earth, the well ran dry and disappeared just as in Egypt. In despair, the people complained loudly to their leader, Moses, that they would die of thirst. But Moses was unable to sing the waters of Creation up from the depths as his sister had. It was then that God told Moses and the people of Israel how to address the well and urge it to bring up the waters of life.

Then Israel sang this song,
Spring up, O well, sing to it.[17]

Slowly they were answered with the well's nurturing waters. Accompanying them to Mt. Sinai where they received the Torah, Miriam's Well remained with them. Its waters caused herbs to grow which the women used as perfume. Soft billowy grass sprouted from its waters which some used to make a bed for the night. But later, when they entered the Promised Land, Miriam's well disappeared. It was thought that it had vanished because they were in their homeland once again and it was natural to drink from other wells. But some missed Miriam's Well and never stopped their search for it. They were the students of the Torah who sought its sustenance in the wisdom of the sacred text.

Centuries later, in the village of Safed in the north of Israel lived the kabbalists—Jewish sages studying the mystical meanings in the Torah. They rediscovered Miriam's Well, claiming that it was found not far from them near the Sea of Galilee. One drink from its pure waters was said to alert the heart, mind and soul and make the meanings of the Torah become more clear.

It was then that water from that well was taken in pouches to wherever Jews had settled. In each generation, it was believed, there lived wise men and women who would sprinkle these waters on the ground and cause new wells to spring forth. Centuries later, the Hasidim of Eastern Europe attested to its ability to reappear, wherever Jews sang to it.[18]

In our own time it is said that Miriam's Well is near those who cast their buckets into any well at the end of the Sabbath as all wells are filled with those refreshing waters at that time.[19] In this way the well now belongs to us Jewish women as we draw up from the depths of tradition the essentials of our sustenance.

In the manner of Miriam after crossing the Sea of Reeds, we have taken up our instruments and begun to sing our songs, to utter the words and tell the stories arising from our longings for the waters of her well. Our spiritual thirst has caused us to search our heritage and the Torah for ways to drink the clear waters of Creation.

The story sparks discussion. Then the women tell other tales they recall: of Miriam as redeemer, prophetess, midwife, singer, dancer, water-bearer.[20] They tell stories and anecdotes heard from mothers and grandmothers and fathers and grandfathers about birth; of their own experiences in birthing their children or helping friends and relatives during delivery. They speak of birth in other contexts: spiritual, intellectual, emotional.
Keeper: We have heard how the story of Pesach celebrates Miriam's powerful voice, a voice which inspires the community of Jewish women to sing and to speak. The Midrash claims that the song of Miriam is unfinished in order to challenge each generation to add to it. How shall we sing Miriam's song now?

Singing:

Woman: This is a song I wrote for my mother who died in the month of *Nisan* like Miriam. Her beautiful music, like a never-ending well, is my inheritance, as is her cacophony.

> "*Kol Shirehah*" (The Sound of Her Song) She sings the song and the rest join in the chorus.[21]

Keeper: "Miriam's Well" is our source of song, of dance, of poetry. "The Well" contains the collective experience of Jewish women, of Judaism and of other peoples. The way Jewish women expressed their triumph at the Sea of Reeds is embodied in Miriam. She is the voice singing in the wilderness above the rest, distinct from her brothers, Moses and Aaron.
That is why we say, "By the merit of righteous women we came out of Egypt." "Miriam" is the collective name given to those Israelite women, our ancestors.
Let's make a *mikveh* of song, a well flowing with music in honor of Miriam. Our voices will be the water in which our souls can bathe.

> Seven women take turns speaking each of the following:
> Water, wells, the Sea of Reeds, the sea of the womb and now a *mikveh* of song.
> Women are like water. We flow together naturally like rivers into the sea.
> We flow from inside to outside to each other.
> We flow with blood.
> We flow with milk.
> We flow with words.
> We flow with song.

Mikveh:

We form two lines facing each other as we sit, and begin humming softly, closing our eyes, imagining that water is pouring through us in the form of sound.

Both lines raise their arms to form a bridge, singing and humming all the while. Eventually one person leaves the bridge to be the "fetus." The "fetus" makes its way slowly through this birth canal of sound. The voices and hands caress this unborn person like midwives, urging her to be born out of Egypt, out of the Sea of Reeds onto dry land. All sound accompanying the *mikveh* is non-verbal.

At the end of the bridge through the "Sea" there is a large bowl of water. The "newborn" sprinkles some water on her face and then the next person embarks on the birth journey, until all have had their turns.

The women's song swells and diminishes, like the waves of the ocean, like the moon in the night sky, like the course of the year and the course of their lives.

After all have "emerged" from the "Sea," we form a circle, dancing and singing. Some use bells, drums, sticks, rattles to accompany the others. Traditionally, the entire *Song of Songs* is sung during *Pesach*. We start practicing on *Rosh Hodesh Nisan*. (See *Elul* for songs from *Song of Songs*.)

We also sing songs of joy and triumph: Miriam's song;[22] *Hava nashirah shir alleluia* (Let's sing a song of Hallelujah! Traditional); *Shiru L'Adoshem* (Sing to God! Hasidic)

The songs and dances gradually wind down and all partake of the food and drink.

IYYAR
APRIL/MAY
A Time To Keep
And A Time To Cast Away

This month's ritual has been designed* with an awareness of our mothers, grandmothers, and great-grandmothers who were earlier inhibited—even in the community of Jewish women—from marking the cessation of menstruation, of *derech nashim* (the way of younger women as in Genesis 31:35) and the release from the physical tasks of childbearing and childrearing. Now wholly freed, our female ancestors would have been ready "to give birth" to their personal creativity, to dip into Miriam's Well without the distractions and responsibilities of family.

As with the Coming of Age ritual in Sivan, which marks a young girl's first menarche, we hope to convey a positive tenor to this life cycle event which has been feared and misunderstood by so many men and women in the past.[2] Once a woman has reached the age beyond which pregnancy ceases, her gender identity is often blurred by society. She is in a transitional state, experienced by those interacting with her as being full of power and danger.[3] During the tumultuous fourteenth century when the Black Death struck in Europe, those women who managed to survive the disease and live to old age were thought to be witches.

In interviewing post-menopausal women to arrive at an appropriate ritual marking their "change of life," I found unanimous reactions. All indicated they would forgo any ritual ceremony that emphasized menopause, fearing a societal backlash which might discriminate against them as they advanced in age. Most said they did not feel very different physically after menopause. The aging process itself was their emphasis; the gradual body changes. These were linked not only to menopause, but to the entire process of aging. Whether these same feelings and attitudes will persist when contemporary young women reach *their* menopause is now being speculated.[4]

Some women may choose to mark the end of menopause with a "mature age bat mitzvah" if they have never had one as an adolescent. Setting a goal such as learning to read and speak Hebrew, to read Torah, to lead a prayer service, teaching a Jewish text within the forum of a bat mitzvah, at an age well beyond 12 or 13, is the way many older women are choosing to re-enter the tradition after years of alienation from, or passive appreciation of, Jewish ritual. Suggestions for a supplementary ritual on a second bat mitzvah, or bat mitzvah post-13, follow this chapter.

Others may wish to invite friends who experienced menopause already or are presently undergoing it. My own mother has said that she could not imagine participating in a menopause ritual, but would have liked to get together with her friends to share experiences of those important years of change.

---

*This ritual for a woman who has reached menopause has not yet been performed. It is hoped that those women who have marked *Rosh Hodesh* each month for several years will be inclined to view this month's ritual content as one Jewish woman's personal expression in coming to terms with menopause. Each woman will find her own way.[1]

Hithbagrut*

Bring: The Book of Ruth (several copies); a group gift for the *mithbogeret.* (As preparation, read the Book of Ruth.)[5]

Setting: Home of the *mithbogeret,* the menopausal or post-menopausal woman, here named Tamar. We are in a sitting room. Have pictures of the woman as a baby, young girl, young woman, bride, mother, grandmother. Flowers and greens of the season decorate the room. Attending are all the female relatives of the *mithbogeret* who can be present—sisters, daughters, mother, aunts—as well as her good friends, including members of the *Rosh Hodesh* group.

Themes of Iyyar
Keeper: *Iyyar* is a transitional month which falls between two major holidays— Pesach, in the month of *Nisan,* and Shavuot, in *Sivan.*

From the second night of Pesach, we count forty-nine days (seven weeks) until Shavuot, the Feast of Weeks. This period is called the *Omer.* When the Temple still stood in Jerusalem, each family would count a sheaf offering of grain to bring to the Temple on the pilgrimage festival of Shavuot. The purpose of this may have been partly a way of blessing the Spring harvest which would also be celebrated on Shavuot.[6]

In the act of counting, the Rabbis saw an opportunity to keep track of an inner harvest of spiritual qualities. Every week of the *Omer* was to emphasize a particular attribute of God. Each day of the week then represented a different permutation of the divine attributes.[7]

In the context of this *Rosh Hodesh Iyyar* marking Tamar's *hithbagrut,* one may think of the counting of years and deeds and events which make up a woman's life. Given are seven distinct stages of life corresponding to the seven weeks of *Omer:* conception, pregnancy, birth, childhood, womanhood, motherhood, and maturity.

In the seven-week counting of the *Omer,* we find the suggestion of seven ritual activities which may be performed during the *Rosh Hodesh* celebration for any given month. We take as our impetus the Rabbis' notion of seven divine attributes to be explored and emulated for the purpose of healing the ills of the universe. We have designated these activities: meditation, ritual immersion (*mikveh*), singing, prayer, storytelling (*midrash*), text study (*talmud torah*), eating and drinking.[8]

Omer as a Period of Mourning
Keeper of *Iyyar:* The period of the *Omer* which includes the entire month of *Iyyar* is considered by observant Jews to be a time of mourning. Wedding ceremonies, hair cutting, and playing music are prohibited. The reasons for

---

*Like *bagrut,* the term used for the young girl's Coming of Age, *hithbagrut* means "maturity, coming of age." However, *hithbagrut* is a reflexive noun, implying a process which reflects a previous maturing process that has been ongoing, a second "coming of age."

this are unclear, ranging from a plague said to have killed the disciples of Rabbi Akiba in the early centuries of the Common Era, to the influence of a Roman superstition which held that during this time of year, the souls of the dead wander into the land of the living.[9]

We do not view menopause as a time to mourn the "end of fertility," as have many in the past. Our purpose in coming together today is, rather, to understand and recognize the meaning of menopause for women who have experienced it or will soon enter its phases. Today we have an opportunity to think of new ways for women to mark this time in future years.

Sign of Iyyar

Keeper of *Iyyar:* The astrological sign of the month is the Bull, *Shor. Nisan* is the month during which seeds are planted. The bull ploughs the earth, bending its broad neck to the ground, dragging a heavy load. The bull tends the change from the new Spring growth of *Nisan* to the first Spring harvest of *Sivan.* The rhythms of the earth reverberate throughout the strong body of the bull.

Kavannah

Keeper of *Iyyar:* In some cultures, once a woman has passed the age of childbearing, she is known as the "Wise Woman" of the community. In her reside the knowledge and values of her people which she transmits to the young. Hers is the status of a venerated elder.

This contrasts sharply with the devalued status of the aging female in our own culture.[10] Today we intend to question this and to learn about the experiences all have had during menopause in order to instill new and positive expectations in our children and grandchildren.

One of the major misconceptions we need to address has to do with sex and the older woman. In Judaism, sex has never been linked only with procreation. On the contrary, in addition to procreation, sex exists for the sake of pleasure, wellbeing, and harmony in a marriage. Therefore, when a woman has passed the age of childbearing and even earlier, she is encouraged by Jewish law to enjoy sex with her partner.[11]

Are there any other *kavannot?*

Each woman voices her own intention for the ritual.

Woman: To mark the passing of physical fertility and to rededicate ourselves to a greater focus on spiritual, intellectual, and artistic creativity and fertility.

Woman: To say good-bye to the womb, *rechem,* the center of childbearing.

Woman: To praise and give thanks for the cycles of life which pulsate through our bodies.

Woman: To say good-bye and good riddance to tampons and sanitary napkins and pads and foams and jellies and diaphragms and pills and anything else I've left out—forever!

Tamar, the *Mithbogeret:* I would like this to be a ritual of transmitting wisdom, *hokhmah.* In Greek, the word for "wisdom," *sophia,* was identified with a female figure. In Hebrew *hokhmah* is a word of the feminine gender. The connection between wisdom and women is clear in Hebrew literature. In the Bible, the wise women of Tekoa and Abel in II Samuel 14 and II Samuel 20, respectively, are examples of what seemed to be a convention in Israel at that time—a woman of the community who knew how to choose her words wisely and communicate the desired message. She was perhaps a female counterpart to the Hebrew prophet, God's instrument of communication with the people Israel. More examples are found in Proverbs 14:1 and in the poem recited to the woman of the household on Sabbath evening, "A Woman of Valor." One of the last lines speaks of her mouth, which "opens with wisdom."[12]

In fairy tales, the woman with special powers, with the knowledge of creation and destruction, is either an evil witch or a good fairy godmother. Both are frequently characterized as older women.[13]

In this *hithbagrut* ritual, we teach and lead a discussion based on two stories of mother and daughter figures where the mother passes on her life's wisdom to her daughter. They are the stories of Naomi and Ruth in the Bible, and Demeter and Persephone from Greek mythology.*

Storytelling[14]

All should have a copy of the story of Ruth and Naomi, or should have read the story in preparation. Tamar, the *mithbogeret,* then tells the Greek myth in her own words.

DEMETER AND PERSEPHONE[15]

Once there lived a goddess who ruled over the earth. She had power over agriculture, causing abundant growth of cereals and grains. In this way she echoed Naomi and Ruth, women of the land. Demeter had one lovely daughter, Persephone, as fair as the first flower of Spring.

One day Persephone wandered far from her mother to pick flowers which beckoned. Steeped in the fragrance of those blooms, she was startled by Hades, the dark god of the Underworld. He seized her and pulled her down to his cold, damp kingdom beneath the earth.

Demeter sank into despair when her beloved daughter did not return. She entered into mourning, forgetting to bring new buds into being. She grieved for her daughter, even refusing to eat or sleep. Thus, the earth was allowed to wither.

When at last she sought aid from the gods to find her daughter, she was told that if Persephone had not eaten food in the Underworld, she could return unharmed to this world. Though Persephone had not been tempted by food, Hades was able to break her resolve with a single ruby seed of a pomegranate. Knowing that if he could induce her to nourish herself in his domain, he could have her as his wife, he strove to make her taste food. Because of that one seed, she would now have to divide her time equally between Hades and Demeter, between the land of darkness and death and the land of light and life.

---

*We suggest that each *mithbogeret* design her own ritual just as in the *bagrut* ritual (*Sivan*). One woman may write a song or a poem, another may wish to teach a text, another may express the meaning of menopause by talking directly about it, sharing her personal experience, her "wisdom" with the group.

That is why the Greeks say that the earth blooms half the year and withers during the other half. When Persephone descends to her husband, Hades, Demeter forgets to bring the buds into being.

Tamar describes the link between these stories in which an older woman passes down special knowledge to a younger woman, and the onset of menopause in which the transmission of wisdom among the members of a women's community is crucial. She tells of her own experience of menopause and asks the other women to share theirs. The younger women who are present share their fears and fantasies of menopause and ask questions of the older women.

Meditation and Movement

Woman: Since menopause involves a new relationship with one's body, we now meditate on ending that segment of our life characterized by an active womb.

This meditation begins with a movement exercise called "Aura-Brushing." The "aura" is the psychic field around an individual. This aura may be affected by fatigue, illness, depression, isolation. The purpose of "brushing the aura" is to symbolize making a fresh start by discarding the cobwebs which drain one of energy.

We start by forming groups of threes, one woman standing in the middle, one on each side of her.

Now the woman in the middle should close her eyes. The other two will begin to whisk the air upward from her feet as they whisper her name repeatedly. They whisk from her feet, her legs, her trunk, up to her neck and head, whispering all the while.

Each woman in the group takes turns standing in the middle while the other two brush her "aura."

Woman: I composed this meditation especially with you in mind, Tamar, as you and I have been working together, I know the kind of imagery you might use for yourself.[16]

It is important to note here that the process just mentioned is a crucial one for the *Rosh Hodesh* ritual. As pioneers in new ritual, we continue to scrutinize our conceptions to create meaningful ceremonies. In this case, Tamar asked for help in saying good-bye to her once-active womb. Another woman might require a different image journey.

Woman: While we composed the following for Tamar, all may participate, even those not yet at menopause. But do not feel you must participate. You may wish to close your eyes, sending healing energy to Tamar. Or, you may wish to start with this visualization and then let your own imagination take over. Some of you may want to leave the room. How you decide to participate is your own choice.**

Now, begin by finding a comfortable position. Close your eyes and focus on your breathing deeply in and out. . . .

See yourself carrying your womb in a crystal jar. Look at it carefully. Take the jar with you to Jerusalem. Carry it carefully up to the Mount of Olives. Find a spot on the Mount of Olives and begin digging a hole with your hands.

Dig deeply, and when the hole is deep enough, place the jar containing your womb deep into the Jerusalem earth. Cover the jar carefully. Know that your

** Some leave, but most stay. Refer to Meditation, p. 113, note 23.

womb is buried safely, forever. Before leaving the spot where your womb is
buried, thank your womb for all that it has given you. Thank the earth for protecting and housing your womb.

Cover the spot with a smooth, white Jerusalem stone. Walk to a nearby
waterfall. Stand beneath it and feel yourself cleansed from within and without.
Return home knowing that you will continue to be creative and productive. Feel
yourself strong and in perfect health.

When you are ready, open your eyes.

When the meditation is over, some of the women share what they felt. Others
remain silent, choosing to listen. Tamar is very peaceful, talking about what this
ritual evening has meant to her.

Gift

The women present Tamar, the *mithbogeret,* with a gift, one they have
made or bought.

The Keeper of *Iyyar* invites all to partake of the food and drink on the
table.

SIVAN
MAY/JUNE
A Time To Honor
The Fruit Of The Seed

From Jewish Girl to Jewish Woman

This month's ritual requires more preparation than other months. The girl who has just experienced her first menstrual period and her mother who is a member of the group should plan together to create a *bagrut,* "Coming of Age" ceremony.

Should the mother attempt to fulfill all her dreams of a Coming of Age ceremony through her daughter, this might become difficult for the young woman. However, when both collaborate in this event, a possible model for later relationships is presented. Further, if the girl menstruates before her bat mitzvah, then the *bagrut* becomes a *kavannah* for her public Coming of Age, the bat mitzvah. However, if she becomes bat mitzvah first, then that provides the *kavannah* for her *bagrut.*[1]

The mother of the *bogeret,* the girl who has "come of age," must be deeply sensitive to the wishes of her daughter in marking this occasion. The mother should be willing to offer support and direction. If the girl is especially shy, this must be taken into account. She should not be urged to do more than what is comfortable. On the other hand, if she is inclined to participate, the mother should encourage the daughter to take the lead. With the help of another mature woman—a best friend, sister, aunt—as an additional mentor, the mother may allow her daughter's creativity free reign.

The Coming of Age ritual is a universal opportunity for the young woman to have her adult status sanctioned.[2] In the confusing stage of adolescence, the young girl's task is to begin to form an identity separate from her family, while not rejecting them altogether. The *bagrut* ceremony allows her to do this—to leave behind her "little girl" status, assume a role in the community of women, and accept the wealth of Jewish tradition.

Bring: The *Book of Ruth.*[3] (During *Sivan* on the holiday of Shavuot, the Giving of the Law, we read the story of Ruth and Naomi.) Mother and *bogeret* should let all know beforehand what will be needed. In this instance, all have been asked to bring a favorite fragrance. Flowers, in the form of a bouquet or a crown, may be used, or a prayer shawl or other ritual object.

Setting: If possible, *Rosh Hodesh Sivan* should be held outdoors during the day, in or near a forest, meadow or park. The group may decide to have this event take the form of a hike and picnic with various stopping points along the way. This is in keeping with Naomi and Ruth who, thousands of years ago, traveled on foot from the fields of Moab to the hills of Bethlehem.

If the group prefers an indoor location, the room can be decorated with Holy Land pictures of Judaean Hills, of Bethlehem, of flowers and trees that grow in Israel, etc. A rug for sitting and greens and flowers can also be added, a custom of Shavuot, the Spring harvest festival.

(The mother of the *bogeret* introduces friends and family who have come to mark the *bagrut* of her daughter.)

Keeper of *Sivan:* For this *Rosh Hodesh Sivan* we shall honor our ancestor, Ruth, who accepted Judaism of her own choice. We will honor her by marking the Coming of Age of Keturah, daughter of one of our group members. Keturah, who is soon to be bat mitzvah, just had her first period last month. Today we celebrate her entrance to Jewish womanhood. It is our custom to accept a young woman into our circle on the *Rosh Hodesh* following her First Blood by at least two weeks.

Themes for Sivan

Keeper: The Giving of the Law on Mount Sinai is a major theme of *Sivan.* We celebrate the Giving of the Law, *Matan Torah,* on Shavuot. This holiday, also known as the Feast of Weeks, takes place on the sixth of *Sivan.* This date coincides with the end of the seventh week after Pesach, when the Giving of the Law occurred.

The story of Ruth reverberates with the theme of *Matan Torah.* Based on the selfless giving of one human being to another, the story of Ruth provides a model in which people live by Torah in a thriving interdependent community.

The month of *Sivan* comes in late Spring, the time of the barley harvest in Israel, the culmination of seven weeks of counting the *omer,* the sheaves of grain grown by each farmer and offered up to God in the Temple in Jerusalem.[4]

The fertility of the earth and the fertility of women are linked in this month, as we know from the story of Ruth. The promise that she would bear children was made by her future husband, Boaz, in his granary among piles of harvested grain from his fields.[5]

This brings us to our main theme of spiritual nurturance. In this month the divine spirit is felt in the maternal, nurturing relationships between people. There is a legend which explains why it is said, "God gave the Torah to the women first." This story emphasizes the power of the feminine spirit. Will someone tell it?

Woman: It was said that when Moses was ready to carry the Torah down from Mount Sinai, God instructed him to utter the sacred words to the women first. Then God explained why.

"First," said the Holy One, "In the Garden of Eden Eve tempted Adam because I had not given her directly the commandment to refrain from eating the forbidden fruit. Therefore, speak first to the women concerning my commandments and the men will heed them.

"Second, women follow religious principles more precisely than do men, so they should be addressed first.

"Finally, the women are the ones who will teach their children Torah. Thus, they must be the ones to hear the Torah first."[6]

Woman: I will add a reason which has been excluded. As women, we instinctively understand Torah. We "hear" it before the men. We bear the Law of Being within us, for we have the potential to bear life. Soon after a boy is born, it is necessary to circumcise him, to put an *ot brit,* a sign of the covenant on his body. A girl needs no such sign put on her. She already bears one within—it is her womb.

The womb symbolizes the repository of the life force, the Holy of Holies where life is sanctified. A baby girl is born with this "covenant of life" in her body. The covenant reaches its literal potential when she bears a child. However, the fact that she has a womb inside her is a constant reminder to her of the equal potential of her physical, spiritual, and intellectual fruitfulness.

Today we are celebrating with Keturah the first tangible sign that her womb is ready to bear children, that she is ready to transmit Torah to the next generation. Today we acknowledge Keturah as a Bearer of Life and a Bearer of Torah. We women are particularly known for our role as teachers of Torah.[7] The majority of teachers in Jewish day schools and Hebrew schools are women.

Sign of the Month

Teomim, twins, is the astrological sign of *Sivan.* There are many pairings at this time, in keeping with this theme. The first is signified by *Matan Torah,* for the sages say that the Torah was God's *ketubah,* wedding contract, with Israel. *Shekhinah,* or the community of Israel as many call her, was "married to God" in this month.

A sacred pairing occurs in human dimensions in the story of Ruth. She weds her fate first to her mother-in-law, Naomi, and then to Boaz.

The twins of *Sivan* are also an emblem of fertility, reflected in the person of Ruth. She produces a child, an heir for Naomi whose sons and husbands have died. She echoes the fertility of the land, productive at this time of harvest.

Puberty Rites at Rosh Hodesh:

The mother of the *bogeret* sets the tone for the day in her own words.

Keturah's mother: Today we celebrate Keturah's coming of age as a Jewish woman. At her bat mitzvah in a few months, we'll celebrate her entrance as an adult into the Jewish community where she will take on the *mitzvot* of learning and teaching Torah, celebrating the holidays, observing the Sabbath. Today, on *Rosh Hodesh Sivan,* we welcome her into the community of Jewish women of the past, present and future.
As the kabbalist, Joseph Gikatilla said:

... in the days of Abraham the *Shekhinah* was called Sarah, in the days of Isaac—Rebecca, and in the days of Jacob—Rachel.[8]

In the days of the Judges, the *Shekhinah* was known as Ruth and Naomi. Here in our community we believe that the month in which a girl's first menstrual flow occurs marks her initiation into womanhood. In the month of *Sivan,* the way Ruth, Naomi and Boaz interacted with each other was thought by the Rabbis to demonstrate the relationship between God and the people Israel, one characterized by mutual caring and trust, by *hesed* or loving-kindness.[9]

This *bagrut* ceremony is also an opportunity for us to reclaim the positive aspects of our monthly flow. It is a time when women separate themselves from the rest of society to experience the vigorous flow of creative energy within.[10] In some societies, women reside in a special hut for the duration of their periods—a way to show respect and awe for the sacred life blood as it passes through their bodies. It is an opportunity for women to share experience and wisdom; to pause in the midst of their daily lives; to reaffirm their sacred capacity each month to bear a child; to recognize their connection with the cycles of life and death which permeate all beings.

A young woman coming of age was probably a major impetus for the celebration of *Rosh Hodesh* in ancient times, before the Rabbis sanitized it by calling it a "reward" for the women at Mount Sinai who refused to donate their gold for the making of the Golden Calf.[11] In our tradition and in our use of a lunar calendar, the link between the cycles of the moon and the cycles of women is understood.

Legend confirms this, telling us that the Israelite women suffered no menstrual pain during the entire time in the desert because they were the first to claim willingness to receive the Torah.[12]

Today we want to change the negative self-image which most of us have known all our lives, the image which the blood taboo has perpetuated. We discard and expel the old notions that we suffer "Eve's curse," that we are unclean, profane and contaminated during the time of our menstrual flow. Today we celebrate our part in the life process as Keturah formally enter our *Rosh Hodesh* circle.

She addresses the *bogeret.*

From this month on, Keturah, we invite you to celebrate the New Moon with us as our female ancestors have done for centuries in different ways.[13] We hope this monthly meeting will remind you that your period is a sacred time of contemplation and rejuvenation. We hope that as you move within the rhythms of *Rosh Hodesh,* you will resist the negativity with which society regards your monthly blood and your womanhood.[14]

Keeper of Sivan: Let's share experiences about our first periods, followed by words of Torah from the *bogeret* and her mother. We'll give special blessings to Keturah along with our gifts followed by singing and refreshments.

Story Sharing:

The Keeper begins with questions:

What do you remember about the first time you menstruated? What had you been expecting? What had you been told? How did your mother, father, siblings, friends react? How did you feel?

The women share anecdotes and stories about their first periods. They remember their mothers' reactions as well as those of people close to them. They remember feeling "dirty" or "special," depending on the "messages" from others. Some imagine how the women in their families in earlier times might have marked their "coming of age."

Torah Study:[15]

Teaching Torah in the form of conveying the deeper meaning of her Hebrew name, is the task which the *bogeret* must fulfill in order to be considered a Jewish woman. Keturah will present a *midrash* based on her name.

Each *bogeret* must find the medium which best suits her interest and nature in order to teach the women something about her name. She can compose a *midrash,* create a piece of visual art, write a song, perform a dance. Her *bagrut* then symbolizes the process by which she takes her name upon herself, as opposed to a passive acceptance. Through the *bagrut,* she finds the qualities she had not seen in her name previously.

In this way, the *bogeret* becomes dedicated to Torah as did her ancestor Ruth. The *bogeret* may look for a word or line in the Torah which contains her name or the root related to her name.

What follows is an example of the teaching of one *bogeret.* However, a *bogeret's* teaching cannot be prescribed, only sketched. (Each *bagrut* must be individually tailored, giving this ceremony deep meaning.)

Keturah's Mother: This *midrash** came to me in a dream when I was anticipating Keturah's *bagrut* ceremony. In it, I found myself before a famous rabbi, asking him, "If, according to Jewish tradition, a man demonstrates his essence, his profound humanity, by performing *mitzvot* (good deeds), then how does a woman show *her* essence?"

The rabbi replied, "By the fragrance emanating from her soul."

Though I knew *keturah* or *ketoret* meant incense, I puzzled over it. How was I to devise a puberty rite from a fragrance?

So with Keturah, I looked for the source of her name in the Torah where her story appears, finding it in Genesis 25—after the death of Sarah, after Isaac marries Rebecca and Abraham takes another wife—Keturah. Nothing except her name is given and the fact that she bore six sons. We also searched the *Midrash* and there we found important clues in our quest for a ritual.

Keturah: First the Rabbis asked why she was named "Keturah." Their answer was: "Because she was *m'kuteret,* fragrant, with good deeds."[16]

The word for fragrance, *"ketoret"* and her name, "Keturah," share the same Hebrew root. That made sense to us, so we arrived at the saying, "Fragrance speaks louder than words." How a person "smells," what he or she exudes, can tell us much, perhaps more than speech. We knew the Rabbis' questions could lead us to a ritual of first menses.

Then the Rabbis asked why Abraham married her. They regarded the wives of the patriarchs as teachers. With Sarah, Abraham had learned patience, empathy, and fairness. He attained a certain level of spiritual develop-

*This provides an example of how one goes about creating a *midrash.*

ment. With Keturah he could go even further as she was "fragrant with good deeds."[17] This is the *midrash* we devised in response to the question: "How should Keturah's first menstrual period be marked?"

(Keturah as narrator reads or tells the story in her own words.)

KETURAH: THE STORY OF INCENSE[18]

A long time ago, in the days before the Incense Gatherers, the fragrance of flowers flew on the wings of the wind. In the Spring, the *Shekhinah* would gather all the flowers of the rainbow and offer them up to her husband.

Sometimes a child was born who would inhale those flowers so deeply that their scent would reach its soul. The child then became like incense, an instrument of communication between the peoples of the earth and the gods of the heavens.

At the time when Sarah, the wife of Abraham, had passed on, there was a young girl, named Keturah, living nearby in a desert valley. Keturah was born to a family of Incense Gatherers, to a tribe which knew and worshipped many gods. Both her mother, Myrrh, and her grandmother, Levonah, had been initiated into the secrets of scent. Keturah, whose name means "fragrant incense," was expected to continue this heritage.

She was a curious young girl who wanted to know why her ancestors had been the incense makers for ritual prayers and sacrifices.

Levonah explained: "Before most of us can remember, there was a terrible drought in our settlement. For some reason, the gods were angry. People were dying of thirst and starvation. Then Reychama, our ancestor, gathered all the spices she could find and offered them up on a fire to the gods, hoping the rains would come. But still not a drop fell. Suddenly, she was driven to throw her body on the fire. Then a wonderful, strong incense floated up from the flames as the rains poured down at last.

"We are the descendants of Reychama, called upon to offer up our incense in an hour of need. Keturah, you are not born with the ability to give forth incense. You must earn it with an act of great courage."

Though the story frightened Keturah, she could not wait until the pungent incense began to emanate from her as it had from her ancestor, Reychama.

Her grandmother, Levonah, continued to instruct her in the ways of the Incense Bearers, preparing her for the day when she would need to give forth her incense. In time Keturah underwent the ceremony of receiving the gifts of her name. This rite occurred the month after a young girl had her first blood. The women of the village honored her with gifts which expressed the meaning of her name.

Then drought struck the village. The plants withered, the animals grew sick and died, the children cried continuously. Levonah prepared herself to be an incense offering in the way her ancestors had prepared themselves, by fasting and praying.

When she was ready, they mounted her on a pyre for burning. The scent of jasmine filled the air—Levonah's scent. Still, the rains did not come. Myrrh, too, was offered as incense, to no avail.

Keturah was numb with grief and rage. This was intended to be an honor? To offer oneself up in flames before hungry gods? She remembered a story Levonah used to tell about a young boy from a neighboring tribe who had tricked his father into seeing that the idols he sold in his store were merely dead pieces of wood and stone, hardly worth worshipping or feeding the choicest morsels of food. A mere boy had stood up against his elders. "An act of courage will free your incense," her grandmother had explained.

Keturah made a vow: "I won't go up in smoke the way my mother and grandmother did. There must be another way. *I won't go!*" She knew her turn would be next, so she fled the settlement, escaping to the desert wilderness. As she wandered further from home, a cinnamon smell wafted from the pores of her skin, leaving an aromatic trail.

Abraham was well over one hundred years old when Sarah died. Isaac had long since gone to set up house with Rebecca. So Abraham found himself alone, still grieving for those he had lost—Sarah, Hagar, Isaac, Ishmael.

One night as he was sleeping, he inhaled a fragrance coming from outside his tent. So strong was the scent of cinnamon, he awoke. He rose from his bed, following it until he found the source—a beautiful girl with dark hair and dark eyes, sobbing. Abraham, known for his generosity, offered her food and drink, the first she had tasted in days. Keturah never returned to her village.

And Abraham took another wife and her name was Keturah. And Keturah bore him Zimran, Yokshan, Medan, Midian, Yisbak, Shuach.[19]

Keturah's Mother: Now let us all come to Keturah one by one, to give her what we have brought.

She leads Keturah to the center of the circle of women where there is a rug on which to sit. One by one, the women approach Keturah, presenting her with the gifts of fragrance they have brought. As each woman comes, she says a few words about the symbolic meaning of the fragrance. Examples follow.[20]

Woman: I've brought you a loaf of dark, whole wheat bread with the smell of soil, leaves and air. Now, as a new woman, this bread represents the earthiness you have, the strength and resilience. (She gives the bread to Keturah.)

Woman: (She gives Keturah a lemon and a pearl-handled knife.) Take this magical fruit. I love the smell of a lemon, an orange, or a grapefruit when it is cut open. I love the pungent explosion. I used to know so many great things to do with the skin of a citrus fruit. I invite you to tear and sniff, to experiment and create, to try new things with old materials. This knife is an old jewel my mother gave me a long time ago, when I was first married. I want you to have it, to learn to cut with it; to cut that which needs to be cut.

(Someone sings: "Lemon tree very pretty and the lemon flower is sweet/But the fruit of the poor lemon is impossible to eat . . .")

Remember, Keturah, the lemon is both sweet and sour. The knife can open up the fruit, but it can also hurt what it touches. This is a way for you to remember the not-so-sweet times and to appreciate them. Bring those times with you into the sweet times, to make for a really full sweetness.

Woman: Keturah, when your mother asked me to bring one of my favorite smells, I thought it would be the smell of woods after rain; very green and mossy, wet leaves underfoot, drops of water hanging from the leaves. I couldn't find it to bring today, so I brought this instead. (Gives her a velvet pouch stuffed with pine needles.) I give you the woods because the trees are rich in meaning. They endure . . . they provide shelter . . . they have deep roots . . . they bend in the wind.

(A woman sings and all join.)

Mi zot olah min hamidbar
Who is this arising from the wilderness

M'kuteret mor u-levonah
Fragrant with myrrh and frankincense

Dodi li va'ani lo ha-roeh bashoshanim.
My beloved is mine and I am his, he's the shepherd in the roses.
(Words from Song of Songs; Music: Hebrew folksong)

Blessings for the Bogeret:

Keeper of *Sivan:* It is time to give Keturah blessings on becoming a Jewish woman.

All: *Atta hu sh'hiktiru avoteinu v'imoteinu l'fanekha et ketoret hasamim.* You are the one to whom our fathers and mothers offered the fragrant incense.[21]

All recite with Keturah the following blessings in Hebrew and English.

Modah ani lifnay ha Shekhinah, may-ayn kha-yay olam, she'mivrati isha, v'notzru bi kokhot hakhayim. I am thankful before the *Shekhinah,* the source of life of the world, who created me a woman and created in me the power of life.

Bruchah at Adonai Eloheinu v'elohei imoteinu v'avoteinu, asher sidrah et halvana b'darka v'sidrah et makhzoray hakhayim. Bruchah at Adonai, she'astani isha. Blessed are You, O Lord our God and God of our foremothers and forefathers, who has set the moon in its path and has set the order of the cycles of life. Blessed are You, O Lord, who has created men and women.[22]

Keturah's Mother: There are special words I want to say to you.

The *bogeret's* mother should now say the words she has prepared. Her remarks need not to be learned or perfectly wrought, but should be heartfelt, expressing what the mother wishes to pass on to her daughter. Here are some possible themes:
—what it means to be a woman;
—what it means to be a Jewish woman;
—what blood signifies.
A sample speech follows.[23]

Keturah's Mother: Keturah, I give you the most difficult and powerful scent I can think of—the scent of your own blood which we are honoring today. I'm going to pour a cup of red wine to symbolize the blood.

Blood is the symbol of life, of the divine spirit which flows through all of us. From earliest times, our people have had a reverence for life. And so we have held blood in awe. We sanctify our food by draining all the blood from the meat, so that we will remember never to take life for granted, never to take the life of an animal unnecessarily, only to take what we must have to eat. As it is written in Leviticus 17:11, "The life of the flesh is in the blood."

Blood symbolizes Israel's coming into being as a nation. Just as you are walking through an invisible door today to accept the challenge of becoming a woman, so the Children of Israel walked out of Egypt, through the Sea of Reeds, into the desert on their way to becoming a free people in their own land.

Just as the leaving of Egypt did not make Israel into a nation overnight, so crossing this threshold today will not make you overnight into a grown woman.

Just as the Children of Israel were not ready to go into the Land of Canaan, so you are not ready to take on the responsibilities of being a mother.

Just as we left slavery in Egypt and took on the *mitzvot,* commandments, so you are leaving your childhood, shaping yourself to be the kind of person you want to be, learning how to become a good parent, an active member of the Jewish community, a strong sister to other women.

Most of the time blood means someone is hurt or very ill.

But this blood of your menstrual period is a cause for rejoicing. A sign of health, not illness; of growth, not death. This blood tells you that you are healthy, that you are growing up according to nature. Eggs were formed in you, Keturah, in *your* womb, even before you came out of *my* womb. Now those eggs have ripened and you are physically capable of having a child on your own.

In the months ahead, that blood will flow and disappear and then flow again, like the phases of the moon when it shrinks to a silver crescent and then grows full and round again. Just so your nurturing blood will fill your womb, ebb, and then fill you again.

My hope is that you will come to accept your own rhythms, to realize that sometimes you will be happy and sometimes sad, that changes and cycles are part of growth, of life. You will soon learn to accept them, even when you are confused or frightened. Now with the onset of your period, you will discover that you have more in common with other women all over the world.

These are some reasons why we meet on *Rosh Hodesh,* at the New Moon—to celebrate the eternal cycles that we, as Jewish women, have in common with the moon, with life, and with each other. You are welcome to come and celebrate with us each month from this time forth.

We Jews measure time by the moon. Like the moon, the Jewish people have gone through dark times and periods of glory. Keturah, may you be perpetually renewed as is the blood inside you, as is the moon, and as are the Jewish people.

Giving of the Gift:
The Keeper of *Sivan* and the rest present the *bogeret* with a gift made or purchased by the *Rosh Hodesh* group. An example follows.

Keeper: Keturah, now that you are woman, you need a tallit, a prayer shawl. When you become bat mitzvah in a few months, you will be able to use this whenever you pray, whenever you want to feel the strength of your Jewish ancestors wrapped around you.[24]

This prayer shawl depicts the thirteen female tribes. With each of the twelve tribes was born a twin sister, and with Benjamin were born two sisters.[25] We each chose a woman and embroidered her into a square—there's Deborah sitting under a palm tree, and Sarah laughing and Rebecca at the well, and Miriam dancing by the sea, and Eve eating the fruit, and Judith with the dagger poised, and Esther seated on her throne and Hannah deep in prayer, and Ruth and Naomi embracing, and Lilith flying through the night, and Rachel weeping for her children and Tamar bearing a child who is the ancestor of the Messiah. The only square left, the thirteenth one, is for you, Keturah, to design and stitch into the center.

> If the *bogeret* has already been bat mitzvah, it is appropriate to recite blessings for placing the tallit on her shoulders.[26]

Keturah: Thank you all. I'll treasure this tallit forever.

> If the group wishes, they can leave the *tsitit*, the ritual fringes which hang from the four corners of the tallit, until the shawl is presented to the *bogeret*. Then all can participate in tying the knots, an activity which is symbolic of the "tying up" or completion of childhood.[27]

Singing:

Two women from the group take the tallit and, holding it over Keturah, they sing and dance around her. All then sing *V'Anu Matsanu Menuchah*,[28] and then songs of childhood and womanhood, cycles and circles.

Sung to the tune of "It Ain't Necessarily So" (from Gershwin, *Porgy and Bess*.)

Eve pulled it down from the Tree,
Yes, she pulled it right off the Tree.
She knew that by eatin'
God's plan she was completin'
So she pulled it right off the Tree.

Chorus:
It ain't necessarily so,
It ain't necessarily so,
The things that you're liable
To read in the Bible
They ain't necessarily so.

Sarah, she laughed when she heard,
Yes, Sarah she laughed when she heard.
A witherin' lady
Could carry a baby,
Sarah she laughed when she heard.

Chorus.

Tamar was a lady of the night,
Yes, Tamar was a lady of the night.
She used all her powers
And worked after hours,
To bring the Messiah to light.

Chorus.

Naomi depended on Ruth,
Yes, Naomi depended on Ruth.
She'd lost everyone—
Then Ruth bore her a son.
Life goes on—he was the proof.

Chorus. . . . End

"Circle Game;"[29] "*Erev shel Shoshanim*"

Eating and Drinking:

The Keeper of *Sivan* and Keturah's mother bring out the "seven species" of the Land of Israel, traditionally eaten on *Shavuot,* the Spring harvest
festival. By eating we strengthen our connection to the Holy Land. We have
wheat bread and barley cakes, wine, figs, pomegranates, olives and honey.[30]
This food which is native to Israel symbolizes the fertility of the earth as
underscored in our reading of the story of Ruth and Naomi as well as by
marking the *bagrut* of Keturah. Other foods symbolic of fertility, such as eggs
and round sweet cakes, can also be served.

We eat and drink until nearly sunset and then we make our way home.

TAMMUZ
JUNE/JULY
A Time To Mourn

An *Avedah* Ritual, Ritual of Loss

Bring: Copies of the story of Hannah; an object of good fortune or protection (a *hamsa* or *mizrach*)* which could be jointly made/given by members of the group to support and strengthen the woman who is the subject of the ritual. (As preparation, read the myth of Tammuz;[1] and the story of Hannah in Samuel 1:1-2.[2])

Setting: At the home of the woman for whom the ritual of healing is intended. Since this ritual will touch upon the very painful issues of loss and grieving, care must be taken to assure that its location is a safe place, free from distractions or noise. Selecting an outdoor area is not encouraged.

Themes of Tammuz
Keeper: The name of this month, *Tammuz,* recalls an ancient myth of death and rebirth—when a descent into the depths is made as a means of fructification. To find traces of the rituals of *Tammuz,* we look in the Book of Ezekiel:

> Then he brought me to the door of the gate of the Lord's house
> which was towards the north; and behold, there sat women weep-
> ing for Tammuz.[3]

According to Sumerian tradition, Tammuz was a beautiful young god or god-like man who died and was then brought back to life with the aid of his sister, Innini. The myth of the dying and rising god, Tammuz, became transformed in Judaism into the destruction and rebuilding of the Holy Temple, the cyclical annihilation and rejuvenation of the Jewish people. This rhythm pervades the history of the Jews.

Several historical events occur in *Tammuz,* marking this month as a time of despair and mourning for the Jewish people. On the 17th of *Tammuz,* Noah sent a dove from the ark to scout for land, but the bird found no place to rest.[4] On the same day, when Moses returned from the top of the mountain, he broke the Tablets of the Law after finding his people worshipping the golden calf.[5] During the time of the First and Second Temples, the walls of Jerusalem were breached by the enemy. The 17th of *Tammuz* signifies the beginning of a three-week period of intense mourning which culminates in the Ninth of *Av, Tisha B'Av,* the date when both the First and the Second Temples were destroyed. That day has since become a minor fast day.[6]

Sign of Tammuz
Keeper: The sign of this month is *Sartan,* the Crab. The crab echoes the major theme of *Tammuz* for it scrapes away at the earth in its search for food,

*Good luck charm, used as protection for the home.

remains buried for a time, and later returns above ground to continue its journey.

Kavannah

Grieving for pregnancy-loss or infertility.

The reader should be aware of the potentially broad applications of the following ritual. In the one presented, the loss is that of a fetus through miscarriage. Our ritual might serve as a stimulus to anyone who has suffered the loss of a child, a parent, a spouse, a relationship, a pregnancy. Society regularly marks the death of a human being, but not necessarily the end of a period of grief. The end of a marriage in divorce,[7] the death of an unborn child, the abortion of a fetus, and the loss of a lover—all require a period of mourning. These events are seldom ritualized. We believe time must be set aside for this.

The following *Avedah* ritual is one example of a woman dealing with a loss which society does not recognize or validate.

Keeper: Tonight, with your help, I would like to perform a ritual to acknowledge an important event in my life. One year ago this month, I lost a pregnancy. My personal loss is reflected in the very character of the month of *Tammuz* during which the life force is snuffed out in the person of the god of vegetation, *Tammuz*. It is also the month in which began the destruction of Jerusalem, the spiritual center of the Jewish people. I, too, lost my spiritual center when I lost my potential child. My very womanhood seemed to be in jeopardy since I could not continue to carry a child.

There are no rituals within Judaism to mark the loss of a pregnancy. For my own spiritual survival, I had to dip into Miriam's Well to create one—based on the story of Hannah in the Bible, in the First Book of Samuel.

Every day since I lost my baby, I have turned to the Book of Samuel to study the story of Hannah, who suffered because she was unable to bear a child. I found solace, inspiration and meaning in her story.

The story of Hannah forms the basis for the *midrash* I wish to share with you as part of my *Avedah* ritual. This *midrash* is about creativity, individual and communal. It illustrates the idea that an individual is often unable to express innermost emotions or thoughts unless other sympathetic people witness them.

I was able to grieve and soul-search on my own, and then felt I needed to come to you with what I discovered, to make a statement as a group about this loss. My hope is that this ritual will heal wounds all of us bear as the result of losses we've experienced.

(A woman starts the ritual by singing a *niggun* and the rest join in. The music sets a mood of sadness, longing, quiet pain and underlying strength. The songs that follow contribute to this mood: *A mol iz geven a mayseh (Yiddish folksong); Gesher Tsar Me'od.*)[8]

Keeper: Let's read the story of Hannah together.

(Copies of I Samuel 1-2 are given. One woman reads the story aloud as the others silently follow. Then a discussion ensues, using these questions. Each group may frame their own or proceed.)

—What is the deeper meaning of the repeated Biblical motif of two wives—
one is fertile and one is barren, one is beautiful and one is ugly, one is
righteous and one is unsavory? Examples are pairs such as Eve and Lilith,
Sarah and Hagar, Rachel and Leah, Hannah and Peninnah, Esther and
Vashti.
—Why is Hannah's prayer considered by the Rabbis to be the ideal form of
prayer? Is this justified? What are your notions of prayer, ideal or mundane?
> After the women have discussed the story, the Keeper explains how she created a
> *midrash* from her own understanding of the text.

Keeper: The stories in the Bible tell of many women who were infertile—they
could not conceive a child. Infertility need not necessarily denote a physical
state but rather a spiritual, emotional or mental state of barrenness. This is
the teaching of Hannah, with its hint as to how one may change the barrenness to creation.

What I did with this story can be applied to any story in the Hebrew
Bible. First, the reading of Hannah's story became for me a daily ritual of
comfort and exploration. Each morning for a year I sat with this story and
digested it, studied it, and was inspired by it. Each day I read another verse
and pondered it, asking questions, struggling with it. Then I read commentaries on the story, mostly in *Pesikta Rabbati,* to see what the Rabbis thought
about Hannah and her rival, Peninnah.[9] Finally I wrote my own version of the
story. It was a synthesis of the original text, its commentaries, and my own
answers to questions about it. Hannah began to speak to me through her
ancient story, through rabbinic teachings, and through my own experience.

This ritual of studying Hannah's story became a *kaddish* which I said
each day for my dead baby. In this way I was able to live through the loss
instead of being consumed by it. The process I have described may be applied to any story which speaks to you in your own situation.

Torah Study:
Keeper: When I looked carefully at Hannah's story, I noted that the turning
point was her prayer. She can no longer tolerate her infertile state and is
driven to "pour out her heart" before God. The text says,
> Now Hannah was praying in her heart; only her lips moved, but her voice could
> not be heard. So Eli thought she was drunk.[10]

Of course, the priest who represented the religious establishment could
not understand such heartfelt prayer and misinterpreted her behavior as in-
ebriation and decadence.

Here, in Hannah's prayerful silence, the text demands of the reader an
active imagination. What is Hannah saying to God? The silent narrative is an
invitation for the reader to open up emotionally, as Hannah did, in order for
inner healing to occur.

This is the basis for the *Avedah* ritual. I'll sing the ballad of Hannah and
when I reach the part about her prayer, I shall stop and invite all to imagine
what Hannah might have expressed.

What would you give to Hannah to help her focus her *kavannah* for this prayer to God, to help her shape her words after her long silence?

This ballad has a chorus with just two words, *Rachem Aleinu*, "have compassion for us." In Hebrew the word for compassion, *rachmanut,* and for womb, *rechem,* come from the same root. I've always thought that the wombs of women form a secret, silent network of communication all over the world. Every woman knows what it means to menstruate, to bear a child, to experience menopause. Every time a woman tells a story "from her womb," other women hearing the story feel it in their depths as well.

Ballad of Hannah[11]
(Tune: Scarborough Fair; traditional English folksong)

1. Once there lived a man named Elkanah,
   "God has gotten" was his name,
   He got two wives, this Elkanah,
   Bitter rivals all the same.

   The first one's name was Peninnah,
   Precious pearl, Pe-nin-nah,
   Mother of pearls, Pe-nin-nah,
   Pearls in her womb, Pe-nin-nah.

   The second one's name was Hannah,
   Full of grace, Hannah
   Full of love, Hannah
   Full of longing, Hannah

   Chorus: *Rachem aleinu* (in cantorial style)
          Rachem aleinu
          Rachem aleinu

   For Peninnah had children while Hannah had none,
   Peninnah had pearls while Hannah had none,
   Peninnah had hope while Hannah had none,
   Peninnah gave life while Hannah gave none.

   Every morning, every day Peninnah would taunt her rival and say,
   Have you fed your children breakfast?
   Have you dressed them for school?
   Have you taught them well the Golden Rule?

2. Hannah spoke not a word in return,
   But deep inside, her heart did burn,
   She thought, there must be more than this to life,
   Than being a mother and a wife.

   Chorus . . . *Rachem aleinu,* etc.

   Years rolled by like unstrung pearls,
   Peninnah kept having more boys and girls,
   Hannah kept waiting for one seed to grow,
   But her belly was filled with darkness and woe.

   Hannah could not eat and she could not sleep,
   All she could do was sit and weep
   And mourn for the children who might have been.
   She felt like a sinner without a sin.

   Chorus . . . *Rachem aleinu,* etc.

   Elkanah tried to understand
   Why Hannah felt like a barren land.
   "Am I not better than ten sons to you?
   Let's count our blessings though they seem few."

   That very year when they went up to pray
   To the Lord of Hosts to bless their way,
   Hannah did remain behind,
   She had words in her heart, she had things on her mind.

   Chorus . . . *Rachem aleinu,* etc.

(The Keeper stops singing at this point and invites the other women to give voice to Hannah's prayer in whatever way feels natural.)

Woman: Hannah, I'd like to give you some words from another woman who knew how to speak from her heart, Emily Dickinson. (She reads "Hope is the thing with feathers.")[12]

Woman: I have a "tune without words" for you, Hannah.[13] My mother used to sing it when she lit the candles on Friday night. I never heard her sing it—she died when I was two. My grandmother, who was not observant, who brought me up, sang it for me as she lit the Sabbath candles. And each time she would say, "I'm only lighting these candles and singing the tune for your mother, because she would have wanted you to know these things."[14]

This is important for you, Hannah, because the Rabbis read into the letters of your name—*chet, nun, heh*—an acronym for the three basic *mitzvot*, commandments, which are incumbent upon women. They are *hallah*, which starts with the letter *chet*, signifying the portion of bread which is to be set aside for the priest each week; *niddah*, which begins with the letter *nun*, meaning the laws of ritual purity a woman is to observe; and finally, *hadlakat nerot*, which begins with a *heh*, lighting candles on the Sabbath, which is the duty of the woman of the household.[15] (She sings the remembered tune.)

Woman: I brought you this purple cord from Rachel's Tomb, Hannah. Brides and new mothers derive strength from the matriarch, Rachel. She also intercedes on behalf of women who have great difficulty bearing children.[16]

By coming together at this time to honor Hannah and Rachel, to think about their infertility and to remember their strength, adding it to our own, we become the "thirteenth stone" for the Tomb of Rachel.[17] This thirteenth stone, forgotten until now, represents the sisters of the Twelve Tribes, the daughters of Rachel and Leah who are here in spirit with us. As the *Midrash* states, "To each of the twelve tribes was born a sister, and to Benjamin were born two sisters."[18]

Now is the time to reclaim the lost stone, the lost words of Hannah, the lost stories of Rachel and Leah and all our foremothers, the lost Torah of the Thirteen Sisters! Let their words resound throughout the land!

The women take turns in reaffirming the meaning of the story.

Woman: Hannah, wisdom grows in your womb like a child. We tell your story on the New Moon of *Tishre,* the greatest *Rosh Hodesh* of the year.[19]

Woman: The Rabbis saw in the letters of the words *Roshei Hodshim* the word *rechem,* womb. The circle of the year is a womb in which the seasons, the earth, the festivals, the sacred stories are born anew, again and again.

Woman: Life can be seen as a series of impregnations, labors, births, growths and then new conceptions, maturations over time. Each "impregnation" may be another coming to consciousness.

Woman: "Pregnancy" may be the stage of carrying an "issue" within, experiencing grief and growth. This is a time of change, confusion, fear, movement.

Woman: "Labor" is the period of struggling with resolution. That may be a painful time or a carefree one. If the birth is healthy, growth continues happily. If the stage of resolution or "birth" is not reached, one may have to begin again.

Woman: Hannah, this way of thinking has helped me. If I can't give birth to a live human being, I can give birth to the ideas and struggles within me.[20]

Woman: Hannah, remember our foremothers, Sarah, Hagar, Rebecca, Rachel and Leah; how they, too, wrestled with barrenness and fertility. Let them teach us how to gain strength through our common struggle.[21]

After the women have offered words to Hannah, the Keeper concludes the story by way of prose narrative and ballad.

Keeper of *Tammuz:* Eli, the priest, was incensed by the myriad voices he heard in the sanctuary. He told Hannah to be gone, to take her drunkenness elsewhere.

But Hannah explained to him that she had not been drinking, saying, "I have been pouring out my soul before God."

Then Eli was struck by her sorrowful, heartfelt words. He had not been able to pray for years and her words opened his heart so that he felt like praying. Her words were pearls, stringing themselves from her heart to his ears. He told her to go back to her husband and tell him what she had just said. Soon, promised Eli, she would have a child.

Hannah returned to Elkanah and told him all she had told the priest. Her husband was overcome by sadness. "Hannah, I never understood your agony at not having children. Tell your story to Peninnah." This was done, and Peninnah, too, was touched by her rival's pains. She embraced Hannah. Soon after Hannah bore a son. Word of Hannah's marvelous gift spread quickly. When people came to tell her their problems, she responded with words which were pearls reaching from her heart to their ears.

Ballad: So Hannah bore many words,
            She only spoke what she heard.
            Inside her grew numerous pearls
            Those words became her boys and girls.

            The first one's name was Shmuel,
            "His name is God"—Shmuel,
            Every word a name of God—Shmuel.
            Every word a pearl—Shmuel.

            Now my story has come to an end
            As Peninnah and Hannah on each other depend,
            For pearls are formed in the womb of grace
            Where the fertile and the barren learn to embrace.

            Chorus . . . *Rachem aleinu,* etc.

The women are visibly moved by Hannah's tale. One woman introduces the concept of group wailing.

Group Wailing:
Woman: I feel that the tears of Hannah are palpable in the air here and so I would like to try weeping together as did the professional mourning women of old.[22]

> She sings a mournful *niggun*, a wordless tune. It is not necessary to have a specific tune in mind. One can begin the group wailing simply by moaning over and over again. This often opens one up to weeping as does the sound of others' moans. This activity will not suit everyone. Those who are uncomfortable with it should be encouraged to remain silent or sit outside the circle. For those who are willing, group wailing is a way to express bottled-up grief in a safe environment. Each group intuitively finds its own rhythm of wailing, rising to a crescendo, a high intensity, and then fading to a *niggun* and to relaxed breathing. A *niggun* in the "blues" mode is very appropriate to this activity. The group wailing ends and there is silence for several moments.[23]

Singing:
The Keeper now sits in the center of the room. The women stand, circling around her, singing songs of fruitfulness and compassion, restoration and rebuilding. As they sing, the woman who is marking her loss may become the center of a final ritual of healing. The women place their hands on her womb, heart and head.

Suggestions for songs: HaNitsamim; Yibaneh Ha Mikdash; Rakhmana D'Anyee (Liturgy—Hasidic melody); Yerushalayim, M'Harbanotayikh Evneh; The Water Lily.[24]

When they have finished singing, refreshments are served. The Keeper has completed the Ritual of Hannah, the climax of a year of mourning.

A V
JULY/AUGUST
A Time To Break Down
And A Time To Build Up

Bring: The Book of Lamentations* in the Hebrew Bible; copies of poems, stories, songs about exile and destruction; a large piece of fabric; four wooden poles for making a *huppah* (canopy); Hebrew alphabet letters cut from colored paper or cloth; needles, thread, scissors; drawing paper, colored pens, pencils; chart of the Hebrew alphabet; *hallot* baked in the shape of Hebrew letters.

Setting: An oasis in the *midbar* (desert), away from the late afternoon sun. Any outdoor or indoor location with added desert associations: a real cactus or photos of Bedouin, camels, red sandstone rock formations, an oasis, suggesting a dry barren place.

Themes for Av

Keeper: The essence of *Av* is contained in its name meaning "father." In Hebrew, it is written *aleph* and *beth.*

During *Av,* we mark the destruction of the Temple in the first and the sixth centuries, B.C.E., by sitting on low stools or on the bare floor, just as if we sat *shivah.* We are reduced to the dry earth and to our beginnings. We rediscover the life process from its origin—the Creation. We shall not fear descent into darkness, into the narrow canyon of the unknown.

But how do we begin when all which preceded us has been destroyed? After the Holocaust, some believed Judaism and Jews had ceased to be. In truth, one chapter in history had come to an end. Now we begin anew from *aleph-bet,* the two letters of the month of *Av.* We find our genesis by initiating a creative process.

Av conveys the themes of destruction and creativity through the holidays we observe during the month. We move from the funereal atmosphere of the destruction of the Temple on *Tisha B'Av,* the Ninth of *Av,* to the joyous mood of *Tu B'Av,* the Fifteenth of *Av,* when the young unmarried women and men of Jerusalem would come to the vineyards and dance. Marriages sprung up like wildflowers from this meeting.[1] With the hope of future generations embodied in this festival, the month of *Av* encompasses the cycle of life to death.

Sign for Av: *Aryeh,* the Lion. *Aryeh* is related to Ariel, the name which the prophet Isaiah gave to the Temple in Jerusalem.[2] The majesty of the lion can be seen as a metaphor for the Temple. The lion is a fierce fighter, symbolizing the endurance of our people.

---

*Refer for preparation. During the hot summer in Eretz Israel in the desert when growth is at a low ebb, one learns to note another concept of fertility—that of mind and spirit embodied in the letters of the Hebrew alphabet.

Kavannah

Keeper: When we think of *Av,* we think of creation from destruction, like vegetation growing from the moist decay that covers the forest floor.
(Each woman offers her own response to this month's meaning.)

Woman: When I think of *Av,* I think of life in death. I remember I became pregnant just after my grandmother died.

Woman: I think of the aftermath of Sodom and Gomorrah.

Woman: Children playing in the rubble of a Jerusalem destroyed . . .

Woman: Rachel weeping for her children . . .

Woman: I think of the questions my parents had after they left the D.P. camps: "How do we start to live again? Is there a Judaism left in which we can participate?"

Woman: I think of my parents' and grandparents' despair and my great-grandparents' hope which formed my Jewish heritage.

Woman: I think of rebuilding the temple in our community, so my kids will want to go there, and their children also.

Woman: Rebuilding the temple, so *I* would want to go.

Keeper of *Av:* On *Rosh Hodesh Av,* let's consider ways we can rebuild the Temple through poetry, story, song, meditation, chanting or building something together.
Keeper: Here is a poem by Katia Molodowsky, a Yiddish poet and novelist who has written much on the Holocaust.[3] (Copies of that and other poems are presented for reading aloud.)

Chanting:

Chanting combines speaking and singing. One woman leads the chant, finding a satisfying rhythm and pace. She then varies the tone, mood and texture of her voice, the others following. She repeats the same verses several times, until the group is silent. The rise and fall of each woman's breathing flows easily into *niggunim* and song.

Woman: Here are verses from the Book of Lamentations: *Al elleh ani vokhiah/ Eyni, eyni yordah mayim* (For these things I weep/My eye, my eye runs down with water).[4]

Other songs are sung spontaneously. (Suggestions: *Hashivenu* (Jewish liturgy); *Al Naharot Bavel;*[5] *Gesher Tsar Me'od.*[6]

Making a Mishkan/Sanctuary:

Woman: I have an idea for building together, using the letters of the Hebrew alphabet.

A *huppah* or canopy symbolizes the Jewish home which a couple builds together. It begins on their wedding day when they stand together under the *huppah* and recite marriage vows. This primitive, portable home also reminds us of the dwellings of our desert ancestors. The first sanctuary, the *mishkan,* which they took on their journey through the wilderness, was a cloth tent.

Here are cloth letters and this large piece of fabric on which to sew them. Let's make our own *mishkan* for Av.

She presents several letters, cut out of cloth, and a needle and thread to each woman. The women begin sewing the letters to the cloth. The group may attach the letters in order of the Hebrew alphabet, or in any other manner, creating a design. As they sew, they tell stories.

Storytelling:

Woman: There's a Hasidic tale which could have been created especially for this month. The Kabbalists believed that the letters of *Av—aleph-bet—* were sacred vessels holding powerful sparks from the time of creation. When the Temple was destroyed, all the physical trappings of Jewish worship went with it. The *Shekhinah,* the Divine Presence, went into exile.[7] The *aleph-bet* the Hebrew alphabet, was all that remained. These letters are our building blocks for the next Temple.

THE SEAMSTRESS' PRAYER[8]

Once there was a poor seamstress who wished to pray to God, but she knew no prayers. Like many of us, she didn't know even a single word of the holy tongue, Hebrew.

"I would like to speak to God," she said, "but I don't know which name to use. I have heard there are many. I would like to give thanks for my life. I know I can't live forever and I wish to say how grateful I am. There are even a few things that do not please me, that I'd at least like to mention."

Then she decided to do what she knew best—stitchery. She knew the letters of the *aleph-bet* which her mother had taught her. With care, she embroidered the letters from *aleph* to *tav* on a plain piece of white cloth. Suddenly the letters moved to form the spoken words of prayer which came from the seamstress. God received these prayers with joy. As time passed, the Hebrew letters continued to form Hebrew words, so that she could utter the thoughts that had been in her soul long before she knew the vocabulary of prayer.

Discussion follows the story as the women continue sewing.

Woman: I have a worse problem than the seamstress'. I know the *aleph-beth* and all the Hebrew prayers, but I can't pray to the God in the prayerbook because He's male. Even though my mother and my grandmother were perfectly comfortable praying to Him, I just can't do it.

Woman: I know what you mean. That's why I'm hesitant about rebuilding the Temple. There were so many problems with the old one. Why do we need a physical structure at all? We have Jewish communities in *Eretz Israel,* and in cities all over the world.

> We talk about these questions: What kind of sanctuary does God require today? Should we rebuild the Temple in Jerusalem? What would be the consequences of rebuilding the Temple?[9]

Woman: I also wonder about Judaism's placing such a high value on literacy, on being to understand and manipulate written texts. This has been the primary domain of men for centuries. The sensual and the tactile, the domain of women who could not read or write, has been undervalued in Judaism.[10]

> A discussion of literacy and Judaism follows. We share accounts of our own struggles to become literate in Jewish texts. Soon all the letters are sewn onto the canopy. Poles are attached to its four corners.

Woman: Before we erect this *mishkan,* let's meditate on our own vision of the new sanctuary. We will begin with a song.

Singing:

Woman: I wrote a song for *Rosh Hodesh Av* about the *mishkan* within. I wrote it as a protection for my spirit which suffers all kinds of hurts, causing it to wither. This song helps me sing my spirit back to wholeness and *shalom;* it brings strength through the words and melody, and through the accompanying movements.

Mishkan[11]

> *Mishkan m'saviv* (a sanctuary surrounding)
> Stretch both arms out to the sides and walk proudly in a slow circle.
> *Mishkan b'kirbi (a sanctuary within)*
> Pull the arms in, bending them around the head, curling the head toward the chest.
> *Hisayon, hisayon p'nimi* (an inner refuge)
> Stand straight and tall in place, eye closed, like a pine tree firmly and deeply rooted in the earth.
> We sing other songs of building, of the Temple, of sacred places: *V'haviotim el har kadshi;*[12] *Yibaneh hamikdash* (Jewish liturgy); *Rozhinkes mit mandlen;*[13] *Va'anu matsanu menukhah.*[14]

Meditation:[15] Building the Temple

Woman: Take a comfortable position, sitting or lying down. Now we shall visualize many things. My questions may help guide your imagination.

Take several deep breaths. Let your entire body relax. If thoughts come in, just watch them go by. Now imagine a desolate landscape. A destructive event has just occurred. There are no signs of life anywhere. Was it a natural disaster or one caused by human beings? What do you see in that landscape? What do you smell? What do you hear? How would it feel to be in that place?

Now imagine the force of life beginning to pulse. Things are starting to grow. . . . Human beings appear. Imagine this landscape of emptiness changing into one of peace and fertility; one which makes you feel strong.

Go to the place. What does it look like? What do you see there? How does it feel?

Imagine you could build a Temple, a place to feel safe. Now, build your Temple, your *mishkan,* from materials you find. What does it look like? How does it feel to walk inside? If you wish, invite other people into your *mishkan*—those who need refuge.

Remain in your Temple and feel the strength flowing through your body and soul. Remember that you are able to return here whenever you want.

(Long pause)

When you're ready, join us in the present, and open your eyes.

When the women finish this meditation, they share their visions of a new Temple. An example follows.

Woman: My *mishkan* was designed on stilts over a mountain, near the water. It was translucent with natural light filtering in. The sound of waves was heard. The *mishkan* was suspended, and I felt as if I were hanging in mid-air. Pillars supported it, and part of it was open, like a *sukkah.* In order to enter it, I had to bow. I came into a room where people sat in a semi-circle, the shape of the new moon. There was Torah study and the singing of psalms.

The problem of *mehitsa** was provided for by cubicles at the back. People could retreat into the cubicles, while remaining physically part of the community—this retreat could happen naturally without calling attention to itself. One could move in or out of the room, yet always have a sense of being under the communal dome.

At the end, we all danced together.[16]

Singing and Dancing:
Second Woman: Let's raise the *huppah* we have made.

One woman stands at each pole, hands clasped around it. The canopy is above their heads, with the letters of the alphabet visible around the edges. The other women weave in and out, around the poles, singing the *Mishkan* song and other music of joy and union, *Yismakhu HaShamayim*[17] and *Halleluyah* (Jewish liturgy). Then, steadying the poles in four support blocks, the women sit beneath the canopy.

Creating with Letters:
Woman: We've built a *mishkan* decorated with the letters of the alphabet. Let's now look at an *aleph* or a *beth,* a *gimel* or a *dalet,* and try to understand what each letter is saying.

The letters have been passed down like precious jewels from generation to generation as a means of communication. The symbols can teach us today, as they have for centuries, how to be creators.

She gives each woman paper and colored pencils.

*Ritual separation of men and women in traditional synagogues.

Take one letter from the Hebrew *aleph-beth* and draw it on the paper before you. Then gaze at that letter for several minutes. Consider the shape and size and color of the letter. Look at it as if you were seeing it for the first time. For those of you who have not studied Hebrew, it may actually be the first time you have concentrated on a Hebrew letter.

What does the letter remind you of? This letter will tell you a story about itself if you focus your attention on it. Sketch the story the letter tells you. What you and the letter communicate is more important than accurate drawing.[18]

> All draw. When completed, the women turn the letters down. Each woman takes a turn telling her letter's story. An example follows, using a brilliant vermilion *aleph*.

Woman: The Bedouin believe that the letters came from formations first seen in the haze of the desert. I'll tell you the story this Aleph brought to mind.

THE ALEPH'S STORY[19]

Once there was a land whose inhabitants seldom spoke to one another, unlike Babel where people tried to understand each other's tongue. As a result, people worked silently side by side but did not celebrate holidays together. While they had offspring in great numbers and traded goods in the marketplace, knowledge of weddings, births, and funerals which had brought families and friends together for generations, now became legends.

Some wandered from place to place, never rooting themselves. The queen of this land remembered her mother's tales of the bustling celebrations of her girlhood. Now none seemed to care. Not a single person came to see the queen—not to lodge a complaint, ask for a simple judgment or beg for the smallest favor.

One day an old man dressed in rags hobbled into the royal court, announcing that he had a gift for the queen. He was turned away, certain that whatever he brought was worthless. But he surprised them, forcing himself in to make his offering. Standing before the queen, he reached into a cracked brown leather pouch, extracting what seemed to be a brightly lit object. Shielding it with his hand so that the queen could behold it without being blinded, he held it out to her.

"This is the most beautiful . . . piece of work I have ever seen. But what is its name?" asked the queen.

(The storyteller now holds up the *aleph* she has made, vermilion and scarlet, red as ruby.)

As the queen held it, it quivered in her hands. "It's alive, but how can it be—it's only a rock!" she exclaimed.

"Is it, Your Majesty? I saw it while fishing. There it lay on the bottom of the stream, gleaming like a ruby starfish."

Said the queen, "First we shall discover what it is, to know how best to use it." Thanking him, the man was given enough food to fill ten pouches before he was sent on his way. Then she called for the most learned men and women of the land. They looked at the strange gift trying to name it. One saw a mirror, another a map of the world, and yet another said it was just a pretty bauble.

When the queen saw her wisest advisors could not decide what to call it, she dismissed them, and proclaimed:

Whoever
has an idea in his or her
head should come to the palace to take a
look at a certain Unknown Object in my possession.
The one who can tell me with certainty
what it is will receive half of all I own.

The response was swift. Many came to behold the unknown object. No two gave the same answer. Soon four who were waiting in line decided to work on the problem. If they were proved right, they would share the prize equally. When they were shown the object, they deliberated among themselves, but produced four different answers, just as had others who preceded them.

Then one had an idea. Sharing it with the other three, they agreed that the first should speak on their behalf.

"Your Goodness," she said to the queen, "is it not true that since this unknown object has arrived, more inhabitants have spoken with you than ever before?"

"Yes," replied the queen, "that is so."

"And, Your Kindness, is it not true that people in your realm have since spoken to each other more than before?"

"True," she agreed.

"Well then, Your Greatness, this unknown object is something sent to those who have forgotten how to speak one to the other. It is actually an instrument called a 'letter,' left behind by the ancient ones. They must have had many such 'letters,' and through each one, people understood much. Each of us here has an understanding of what the 'letter' means. There is not only one correct meaning but many possible ones. Let us not have all agree, but rather encourage the debate to continue."

The queen decided to give the wise woman and the other three half of all her property. The unknown object was copied and displayed everywhere. People came singly and in groups to look at it and challenge each other's visions and versions. Thus, all began to speak together and to meet together again, as in the old days.

When each woman has told about her letter, one brings out the *hallot* in the shapes of the letters of *aleph* and *beth*. *Av* smells like a warm oven. With strong baker's hands, the woman clasps the breads together and blesses them.

Woman: As we eat this bread which has come from the earth to nourish us, so may we nourish others with the food of our souls.

All say *HaMotsi*, the traditional blessing over the bread. The letter-bread is offered and all eat. Other foods are brought out, fruits of summer and cold drinks. The desert sun is setting at last.

E L U L
AUGUST/SEPTEMBER
A Time To Embrace

A Pre-Wedding Ritual: Friends of the bride, her mother and future mother-in-law may be invited. Each participant should consider a gift symbolizing a new beginning, or a spiritual idea wished for the bride in her new marriage.*

Bring: *Huppah* or large decorated umbrella; musical instruments—tambourines, bells, drums, recorders, sticks; a gift from the group.

Setting: A place near the water or wherever possible to wash, dip, bathe; may be a beach at an ocean or lake, an indoor or outdoor pool, or an outdoor shower. Participants may bring bathing suits. If no water is available, a large bowl filled with water may be used as in the chapter on *Nisan* (April/May).

Themes for Elul
Keeper: According to the sages, the name of *Elul* is an acronym forming the first letters of the words—*Ani L'dodi V'dodi Li* (I am my beloved's and my beloved is mine). In Hebrew the letters would be *aleph-lamed-vav-lamed.* Perhaps after all those matings of *Tu B'Av, Elul* became the month for weddings.

In *Elul* we start to prepare for the New Year which takes place in the following month, *Tishre.* The New Moon of *Tishre,* Rosh HaShanah, is the day on which we celebrate the creation of the world and it is customary to think of the 25th of *Elul* as the beginning of the "week" of creation. *Elul*—a month of anticipating the creation of the world.

We could think of this month as the time when God's love is manifested through the creation of the world. In *Sivan,* God united in sacred marriage with the Jewish people. In *Tishre,* God became "wedded" to the world. In *Elul* we celebrate this with songs of love, melodies from the Song of Songs.

From *Rosh Hodesh Elul* until Rosh HaShanah, we blow the *shofar* each day to reawaken us in preparation for the turning of the year.[2]

Sign of Elul
Keeper: *Bethulah,* the Virgin, is the sign of *Elul.* We use "virgin" in its original sense, meaning "independent of a man." It seems contradictory then to be celebrating the coming together of a woman and a man this month. But this is appropriate today when women of all walks of life, of all ages, of every sexual preference, must still struggle with how to grow free of the rules, traditions, and values of men.[3]

Therefore, one purpose of this pre-wedding rite is to strengthen and reaffirm the commitment of the women's community to the bride, Batya, and to help her find ways to be a "virgin woman" as well as a married woman. Thus, the bride's community provides the context within which she constantly struggles with her status as woman and Jew, within marriage and a relation-

*Please turn to note 1 for further preparation.

ship, and as a biological and spiritual mother. The ritual we are about to perform signals to all women present that it is our right and obligation to help Batya maintain her individuality as she deepens her commitment to her partner.

"Virgin" also represents a state of purity akin to that attained at the season of the High Holy Days, when our souls are renewed. The virgin month of *Elul* is, itself, a *kavannah* for the New Year.

Kavannah
Keeper: What we are doing today is in the tradition of the wedding shower, with a difference. We have not gathered here to make the bride-to-be rich in material gifts. Rather, we want to add to her spiritual wealth before she sets out on the long road of marriage. Since *Elul* is a month of spiritual readiness and preparation for the renewal afforded by *Rosh HaShanah,* we shall prepare ourselves and Batya, the bride-to-be, in a communal rite of purification, a *mikveh.*[4]

This pre-wedding rite might have been done by our traditional great-grandmothers or even our grandmothers.

Woman: Except for the part about the ocean. I doubt that our ancestors in the *shtetl* used to have pre-wedding parties by the ocean.

Woman: But other Jews might have done something similar. Jewish women of North Africa and oriental countries customarily held a party for the bride at the *mikveh* the day before the wedding.

Woman: I've always wondered how the oriental women came to have such a unique ritual tradition.

Woman: It seems one cause was their interaction with Arabs in Arab society, where women live mostly in separation from the men. They learned from Arab women, borrowed from them, learned their songs and recipes.
They were often obliged to improvise songs and stories because they were illiterate and could not penetrate that portion of Jewish tradition which was bound to the text. All their creativity went into spontaneous expressions of joy and sorrow, depending on the occasion.

Kavannot:[5]
Woman: Batya, I was married before and so I know what it means never to reach oneness with another person. I was completely alone in my marriage. I pray for you to find the real meaning of *da'at,* knowledge, with your husband-to-be; the way Adam and Eve "knew" each other, not only in the flesh, but in the soul.

Woman: You are much younger than I, Batya, and yet much more aware of your "sparks," your potential, than I was at your age. Twenty years ago I was hopeful of union, of family, of coming to live in Israel with the right man.

Standing under the *huppah,* we were two people, identified with each other's dreams and aspirations.

I didn't realize then that we would always be separate, that we would touch sometimes, but never successfully join forever. When you meet the soul which matches yours, there's a great temptation to want to be one—in every way—especially in this world where each step towards *tikkun,* regenerative energy, is very precious. Batya, I hope you and your husband can learn the dance of uniting and separating, to be partners and individuals at the same time.

Storytelling:[6]

Woman: I'd like to tell a story in Batya's honor about the traditional Jewish notion of a "match," so we can contrast it with current ideas of marriage. Written by the Yiddish author, I.L. Peretz, whose life spanned the nineteenth and twentieth centuries, this is a Jewish version of "Cinderella."

A summary of the story follows. For a fuller version, see Note 7. (Another story or reading appropriate to the group and to the bride may be substituted.)

THE MATCH[7]

Two families in distant parts of Eastern Europe are very anxious to find matches, one family for a son, one for a daughter. Through the mystical powers and womanly intuition of Sarah Bas-Tuvim,[8] the young man and woman are guided to each other. Sarah Bas-Tuvim gives the man a shoe which fits only the young woman's foot. In true Cinderella style, the pair are married and live happily ever after.

The women discuss the story, some reacting with anger and criticism, some questioning the old notions of marriage and love which are portrayed, some finding comfort and rationality in the traditional values set forth.

Questions for discussion:

—What is Sarah Bas-Tuvim's message to the bridal pair?

—What is your concept of the ideal marriage or union?

—What is the Jewish concept of marriage and what are your opinions?

—How do you know when you are ready for marriage and commitment?

The women tell stories of their own weddings, and others they have attended.[9]

Keeper: I witnessed this scene last summer in Jerusalem when I attended a wedding in the Jewish Quarter of the Old City. It took place at midnight under the full moon on a Jerusalem rooftop only a few steps away from the *Kotel,* the Western Wall.

The bride was being marched around the groom seven times; however this bride was *leading* her escorts—with strength, direction and surety—very certain of her part in this "unioning." Taking full charge, she was singing— louder, perhaps, than any of us who were witnessing the event. How strange to hear the voice of the bride under the *huppah!* The bride is traditionally silent, her part in the ceremony being one of acceptance, silent and secret, yet here was a *singing* bride, one taking the lead role.

I thought of the song, *Od Y'shama*, (Jewish liturgy) and the inspiration for this walking meditation* came to me.

Meditation:[11] The Circle of Sound

As the women stand in a circle, the leader sings and all join her: *Od y'shama b'arei Yehudah* (Let there speedily be heard in the cities of Judah)/*U'vekhutzot Yerushalayim* (And in the streets of Jerusalem)/*Kol sasson v'kol simkhah* (The voice of joy and the voice of happiness)/ *Kol hatan v'kol kallah* (The voice of the groom and the voice of the bride).

They sing the song several times and the keeper instructs them to walk slowly in a circle, still singing, then to omit the words to the song and substitute "la-la-la." She leads them, walking very slowly, singing the melody. She then moves toward the center of the circle.

Keeper: As we form a spiral walking and singing, we also offer a prayer for redemption . . . with the steps toward that redemption becoming ever more determined. . . . From the outer cities of Judah . . . to the inner city of Jerusalem. . . . From the outer sound of joy . . . to the inner sound of happiness . . . from the outer voice of the groom . . . to the innermost voice of the bride.

How heartfelt is that moment when the bride reclaims her voice of joy and happiness under the *huppah.*

Let's stay in that spiral now, still and silent, thinking of how we want to bless Batya later. All stand silently for a few moments, eyes closed. Then the keeper begins humming "*Od Y'shama.*" As the women open their eyes, she leads them out of the spiral and back into a circle.

Keeper of *Elul:* Let's enter the water now and say the blessings of purification together.[12]
She steps out of the circle and takes off her clothes, inviting the women to do so. Those who wish to wear bathing suits or other attire may do so. All walk to the edge of the water.

Purification by Water/Mikveh:[13]

Woman:

At the first moment, when God created heavens and earth, the earth was the depths and God's spirit imbued the waters. Then God separated the waters, above and beneath. (Genesis 1:1-8)

Like the separation of the waters, we distinguish between one moment and another in the flow of time. In some moments we are conscious of transformation and re-enter the waters of separation for renewal.

Welcome us Holy One

As we enter Your life-flow

Surround us

Support us

Carry us to new shores

Reflecting and altering our consciousness of our act of immersion, we say two *b'rachot*, blessings, to separate the moment.

---

*"Walking meditation" is a universal form of inner contemplation brought on by the simple act of walking carefully and slowly. This may be the essence of the traditional bride's walk around the groom seven times under the *huppah*, a way for the bride and groom to focus on their union through movement.[10]

The first is: Holy One of Blessing, Your Presence swells creation with the waters of life.
All walk into the water together.
The second contains the Shehechayanu, using its recognition of our threefold
relationship to God for each of the three traditional immersions: (While dipping)

Shehecheyanu: the life-force which flows in and through us.
Vekiyamanu: the trust and sustenance on which we rest, and can allow ourselves
to float.
Vehigiyanu lazman hazeh: the movement which carries our lives onward in time.
(The women emerge, dry themselves and dress, returning to the circle.)

Blessings for the Bride:

Keeper of *Elul:* Now that we have purified our souls in meditation and our
bodies in water, let us bless the bride under the *huppah* we have brought.
This is a preparation for the next week when she meets her beloved under
the canopy. There she will receive many more blessings.[14]

Several women erect the *huppah*, which may be an actual canopy or a large decorated
umbrella. They hold it over Batya's head. The others stand around her. One by one, they
approach her, whispering special blessings in her ear. One woman recites a poem she has
written for the occasion.

The Wedding[15]

Friendship's full circle wraps
Prayer shawl of sunlight
Over majesty's arms

Beauty weaves garlands
With whispers of G-d's prayer
In chorus of song

While under the *huppah*
We dance with angels
In seven time rounds

Singing and Chanting:

Because the name of the month, *Elul,* signifies a
pledge of love—*Ani l'dodi v'dodi li*—the women sing songs of love and chant
verses from Song of Songs as they stand under the canopy. *Song of Songs* is
full of sensual poetry to chant together or individually.[16]

Chanting leads naturally into singing: *Dodi Li V'Ani Lo (from Song
of Songs, traditional); Iti m'Levanon* (traditional); *Kol Dodi Hiney
Zeh Bah* (traditional); *Et Dodim Kalah* (trad.); *Ani L'Dodi*[17]; I Know
Where I'm Goin'[18]; Lavender's Blue.[19]

The poetry and melodies spark memories which the woman share with
each other. They speak of their sexual experiences: the first time they made
love; changes in their attitudes toward sex over the years; the learning and
omissions about sex from their mothers and sisters.

Blowing the Shofar:

Woman: During *Elul* it is customary to blow the *shofar* to usher in the New Year in *Tishre*. The sound of the *shofar* proclaims renewal for the world, for the year, for the Jewish people. I've brought a *shofar*. Let's take turns blowing it to usher in the coming year.

> She blows several long notes and passes it on to the next woman. Each woman tries, with varying degrees of success . . . some have never tried to play it before. Instructions for blowing the *shofar* follow.[20]

Woman: *Kavannah* is very important for *shofar*-blowing. Approach your instrument positively. Say to yourself, "This is going to be fun—I can't wait for the sound to come right out."

First, contrary to popular misconception, *don't* puff your cheeks. Next, purse your lips, as if you were about to say "P".

Now, bring the mouthpiece of the *shofar* to the center or side of your lips, whatever feels more comfortable. Purse your lips. With a strong tongue thrust placed behind them, SPIT, emitting spurts of air through a very tiny opening.

Finally, push your wind through the *shofar*. Let it flow and fill up the space around you. Exclaim *Amen Selah* under your breath.

Dancing and Music:

The bride-to-be has a flute, recorder or other instrument which she plays as she walks. The women follow her, then dance around her doing simple circle dances such as the *hora*. When the bride stops playing, she joins the others.

As the dancing winds down, the Keeper of *Elul* leads the group to the refreshments, snacks of fish and eggs and green vegetables which symbolize fertility, as well as sweet cookies, cakes and wine which portend a sweet life for the bridal couple.

PART III.

Starting A Group

Addenda

Notes

Bibliography

Starting a Group

If what we have written thus far stimulates you to start your own *Rosh Hodesh* group, here is a step-by-step plan:

Forming a Core Group
A major tenet of the *Rosh Hodesh* revival is shared leadership. There is no single rabbi; instead, women take turns coordinating a monthly meeting.

If two or three other women wish to plan, all the better. If you are on your own, invite several interested women you know to attend the first meeting. In this way, you can encourage participation, because you will know their specific talents. If you know a woman who likes to lead singing, you already have an invaluable participant for the first meeting.

Announcing the Get-together
Contact prospective group participants as to the date and time of a first *Rosh Hodesh* celebration. Include women of all ages, all walks of life, all degrees of Jewish involvement. Variety will make for a group of diverse interests, talents, and concerns. Don't hesitate to invite many more women than you hope will attend. First meetings are often quite large. By the second and third meetings, however, the group will settle down to a reasonable size. With ten to fifteen regular participants, there is ample time and space for each person.

See the sample invitation, p. 110.

Studying the Month Together
The rabbis of the Talmud did it all the time! Studying in *hevruta,* with a partner, is essential to the Jewish learning process. It is the custom of women who celebrate *Rosh Hodesh* to meet together in a small study group of two to four to prepare for the month.

According to tradition, it is a *mitzvah,* a sacred command, to study upcoming holidays a month earlier, bringing the occasion closer and setting the mood.

Study the themes of the month found at the start of each chapter and brainstorm. Consider the season in which the month falls, as well as the astrological sign of the month. Read about the important Biblical events as well as events in Jewish history which occurred in the month. Find all the *midrashim,* stories about particular Biblical figures who were active in that month.

Once you are all familiar with the content and character of a month, list activities for women's participation. We think these seven ingredients comprise a successful *Rosh Hodesh:*

1) Song/*Niggun*[21]*
2) Story/*Midrash*[22]*
3) Meditation/Visualization[23]*
4) Dance/Movement[24]*
5) Text Study/*Talmud Torah*[25]*
6) Food[26]*
7) Purification of the Spirit/*Mikveh*[27]*

Prepare familiar music about the season or holidays of the month. Find a story about a Biblical personage associated with the calendar month. You may not wish to use all seven activities, or you may discover additional ways to add to the above techniques.

Kavannah[28]*

In order to arrive at a list of suitable activities for the *Rosh Hodesh* gathering, it is often helpful for leaders to focus on important directions and lessons of the month. For example, in the month of *Av* (July/August) when the Temple was destroyed, a *kavannah* for the group could be identifying with the Jews of that period, understanding the loss of one's spiritual center.

The leaders might read accounts of the destruction of the Temple, the Book of Lamentations, and selections from the literature of the Holocaust. One woman might compose a guided fantasy about rebuilding the Temple. Once the *kavannah* or desired focus for the month is clear, activities seem to flow naturally.

The First Meeting

We suggest a two-hour meeting, where women will get to know each other. Creative rituals do not happen instantly; but after much time is spent together, getting acquainted through shared activities and joint study.

Start by self-introductions in a circle, giving your Hebrew name and its meaning, if known, and the person you were named for. Another good opening activity is to tell anecdotes about a Jewish woman you admire greatly and why. (See *Heshvan,* October/November.)

Distribute a Jewish calendar as a guide to the months so that those who are unfamiliar with the Jewish yearly cycle will have a ready aid. (See our calendar p. 4-5.)

Ask those present to share their expectations for the group. Have someone record these ideas for future reference and direction, or simply tape-record the session. The path of the group comes from the individuals in it, and *not* from a leader's preconceived notions.

*See Notes, Part I; also Key Terms, p. 16

Use the talents of the people who come to the meeting. Often, it is a good idea to ask who has brought ideas, activities, songs, stories for the evening. Then the Keeper of the Month, the hostess for the meeting, can invite those women to use their talents when the time seems right.

The Keeper is responsible for setting the stage, explaining the basic themes of the month, and inviting others to lead activities. Beyond that, it is up to each group member to take responsibility for infusing the *Rosh Hodesh* ritual with life. Think of the first meeting as an improvisational rehearsal for a performance whose script is still in the process of being written. The *Rosh Hodesh* ritual is a play with a constantly changing script, players, setting, mood and intent.

The Next Meeting

Before the first meeting is over, set a date and place for the next one. Because the New Moon does not fall on the same day of the secular calendar month each time, you may not wish to meet on the actual day of *Rosh Hodesh,* the New Moon. We meet anytime up to fifteen days into the month, the time when it is still permissible to do *kiddush levanah,* the sanctification of the New Moon.[29]

Our custom is to have the woman in whose house we meet coordinate the meeting. She need not lead it all by herself; rather, she is responsible for making sure that enough people have brought "ingredients" for the ritual to begin its "cooking."

L'hatslacha—To your success!
Rosh Hodesh Sameach—Happy *Rosh Hodesh!*

---

date

Dear Friends,[30]*

Jewish women have been celebrating the new moon, *Rosh Hodesh*.
"The beginning of renewal" is welcomed by small communities of women
who sing, teach, meditate, learn and eat. Most important, they come together
as women with shared interests in active Judaism.

We are writing to invite you to a *Rosh Hodesh* celebration of a group
being formed. As we welcome the new moon of ____(name of Hebrew month/
English month)____ , we shall explore these questions:

As we seek religious equality, should we emulate male rituals or explore uniquely feminine rites? What might that mean? Can we create authentic ritual?

How can we deepen our awareness of natural cycles and rhythms in this
age of the digital clock?

The new moon of ____(Hebrew month)____ will be celebrated at the home
of (name and address) _____ at ____(time)____ on ____(date)____ . Call
____(phone #)____ for directions.

How to Prepare for *Rosh Hodesh*: think about the time of year, how it
makes you feel, what is going on around you in nature and in the lives of
those you know. What are the Torah readings for the month? What is the
astrological sign for the month?

Rosh Hodesh rituals have many styles, depending on those who come
and what they bring. That is the key to *Rosh Hodesh*. Bring with you a
thought, a hard-earned insight, a story or a song, an instrument . . .

Rosh Hodesh is open to sisters of spirit. Please extend the invitation.

---

name of sender

*p. 114

ADDENDA: PERSONAL PARABLE

Aviva's "Origins of Rosh Hodesh*":*

First came the sixties. But the sixties didn't reach Minneapolis until the seventies. At that point, the women's movement and the awareness of "Here I am for everybody's rights, women rights and minority rights" was strong. Still, I was leaving out part of my own identity. Jewish rights and women's rights came to my consciousness around the same time in the mid-70's. Shortly after these two ideas came together for me, I realized, to my great dismay, that they conflicted according to dogmatic feminist terms and orthodox Jewish terms.

In Judaism, there is a division of labor for the effective functioning of society: men function in a social sphere and women function in a family and supportive sphere. Feminism is trying to equalize that division, or at least provide choices. That's where the tension has developed.

As all this turmoil was going on in my life, there was a lady named Darlene Marvey who was having the same kinds of conflicts regarding the interactions of feminism and Judaism in her own life. She had resolved the conflict by saying, "It's not that there aren't strong Jewish women. There are—they simply are not talked about, known, or studied. So let's do that."

She put together two groups to study the seven prophetesses (according to the Talmud there were seven): Sarah, Miriam, Devora, Hanna, Hulda, Esther and the other foremothers—Rachel, Rebecca, and Leah were all included as one entity.

We began to study, using traditional and modern commentaries on the Bible. Then Darlene said, "We're working in one sphere towards resolving our conflicts about being women and Jews. But let's not just study, let's celebrate.

She then invited women from both groups and told us to bring other women who might fit in. We came to her house on Rosh Hodesh to celebrate. She invited us with the clear understanding that all of us had to bring something. People brought musical instruments and stories and songs and food and dances and ideas. I remember feeling like we were making a declaration of independence. It was a combination consciousness-raising group and religious event!

Ever since that time, I've been making Rosh Hodesh each month. When I moved from Minneapolis to Philadelphia, I brought the ritual with me. And that's how it all began.

NOTES FOR PART I

(Complete citations for authors in Bibliography, p. 137)

¹ Information on the Jewish calendar is from Cohen-Kiener's unpublished paper, "Astrology and the Jewish Calendar," 1982.

² Schauss, *The Jewish Festivals; Encyclopaedia Judaica,* Vol. 5:43-54; *"Piska 20,"* in *Pesikta Rabbati* for meanings of the signs of the zodiac in the context of Judaism.

³ See James Pritchard, *Ancient Near Eastern Texts,* pp. 62, 80, 83, 188 and Levow: See numerous articles by Ezra Fleischer in the Hebrew journal, *Tarbiz* from 1968 onward on the ancient celebration of the New Moon; see Avram Arian, "The Evolution of *Kiddush Ha-Levanah,"* Hebrew Union College Thesis, New York, 1976.

⁴ See "Origins of *Rosh Hodesh"* in *Heshvan.*

⁵ Ginzberg, Vol. 3:122.

⁶ "Text" is used as in contemporary folklore scholarship: any cultural artifact or material may be examined, as a literary text is examined for meaning.

⁷ Barbara Myerhoff, *Number Our Days.* (N.Y.: Dutton) 1978, p. 240.

⁸ Genesis 35:16-17.

⁹ *Genesis Rabbah* 82:8

¹⁰The discovery of the *midrash* of the thirteen sisters was made by Rabbi Cynthia Kravetz who was listening to a *d'var Torah,* a learned discourse on the Torah at the Germantown Minyan in Philadelphia in 1980.

¹¹See Part I, p. 3 and Adar Aleph section, Themes, for an explanation of why there are sometimes 13 months in the Jewish calendar.

¹²Schauss, *The Jewish Festivals,* p. 181.

¹³*Encyclopaedia Judaica,* Vol. 11:1234; Tractate *Sukkot* 5:2, 51b-52a.

¹⁴*Encyclopaedia Judaica,* Vol. 15:501-502.

¹⁵The notion that words uttered in a sacred context have sacred qualities, is discussed in Alfred Lord, *The Singer of Tales,* (New York: Atheneum, 1965) and in Dan Ben-Amos, *Sweet Words* (Philadelphia: ISHI, 1975).

¹⁶Woolf, *A Room of One's Own.*
The Hebrew concept of the sacred comes to bear on our definition of "womanspace." The word for sacredness, *kedushah,* comes from the root *Kaf-Dalet-Shin* which means "to set apart." In Judaism, to sanctify existence is to make distinctions.
The Creation story illustrates this. The first distinction was between darkness and light: "God called the light Day, and the darkness He called Night." (Genesis 1:5). There followed in swift succession distinctions between dryness and moisture—"God called the dry land Earth, and the gathering of waters He called Seas." (Genesis 1:10); between the sun and the moon—"God made the two great lights, the greater light to dominate the day and the lesser light to dominate the night, and the stars." (Genesis 1:16); between fish and beast and fowl—"God created the great sea monsters and all the living creatures of every kind that creep, which the waters brought forth in swarms; and all the winged birds of every kind." (Genesis 1:21); and of course, the distinction between male and female.

In Orthodox Judaism, the distinctly separate roles of the sexes are intended to preserve the balance of the universe.

[17]See Agus, Cantor, Schneider; Levow (doct. diss.) and materials of the Jewish Women's Resource Center, NYC and the Women's Institute for Continuing Jewish Education, San Diego.

[18]Aviva Cohen-Kiener, Interview by Suri Levow Krieger, Philadelphia, January, 1981. For a complete version of her statement of the origins of the ritual, see Part I, Addenda.

[19]For a study of current witchcraft groups in the United States and societal implications of this movement, see Adler, Margot.

[20]See Gilligan, pp. 5-23.

[21]A *niggun* is a melody without words. The Hasidim have a rich and varied tradition of singing, chanting, and humming as a form of prayer. See *Encyclopaedia Judaica,* "Hasidism," Vol. 7:1422-1426 and I.L. Peretz, "Migrations of a Melody" in *Stories from Peretz.* Sol Liptzin, ed. NY: Hebrew Publishing Company, 1947, pp. 157-176. In the context of a Rosh Hodesh celebration used to unify the beginning group; as a bridge from one activity to another, to achieve a contemplative mood, and at the start/or end of a meditation.

[22]*Midrash* comes from the root daleth—resh—shin meaning "to seek" or "inquire." A midrash is an interpretation of a text with a strong element of creativity included. A famous example is the midrash about the infant Moses and the burning coal. This story is to be found nowhere in the Biblical text; however, it is very closely associated with stories of Moses' growing up which are in the Bible. This midrash is a teaching device which answers the questions: Why did Moses stutter? Why was Pharaoh afraid of Moses? How do we know that Moses was destined to lead the Jewish people?

In Rosh Hodesh gatherings, *midrashim* are frequently used to explain the gaps in our knowledge about Jewish women, especially those in the Bible. For more on *midrash*, see p. 15. For examples of Jewish women experimenting with the midrashic form, see *Taking the Fruit: Modern Women's Tales of the Bible.* (San Diego: Women's Institute for Continuing Jewish Education, 1981).

[23]Meditation and visualization ("image journeys") are often the climax of a Rosh Hodesh event. Meditation represents the epitome of *kavannah* for the month. Meditation with *niggunim* can start the ceremony. Usually we sit in a circle with eyes closed, listening to our breathing for a few minutes before starting New Moon activities. (It is essential to start the meditation with relaxation exercises—deep breathing, stretching, etc. though these specific instructions are not mentioned each time.) Then someone suggests we direct our thoughts to the month ahead, what it represents to us, to the Jewish people, to the natural world.

In the middle of the ritual, after we have discussed themes of the month; told stories, sung songs, meditation can deepen our understanding. (Once during Rosh Hodesh Av, Benji Jackson-Danniker of Boston led a meditation based on wisdom she had received from her grandfather about the rebuilding of the inner temple)

Meditation can also be used for healing—based on the idea that the moon which has been hidden reveals its light at Rosh Hodesh, thus opening ourselves and to each other's relationship, focusing on the person to be healed or given strength, chanting that person's name, visualizing images of power, wholeness, peace, health.

For more on Jewish meditation, see Chaim Rosen, "Jewish Meditation," *Wellsprings,* Jan./Feb. 1985, Brooklyn, NY: Lubavitch Youth Org., and Kaplan.

[24]For dance and movement, we blend modern, improvisational and Jewish folk dance. Your local Hillel or Jewish community center offers such dance instruction.

[25]For text study ideas and how to begin, see Siegel et al., 1973, pp. 289-295. Your local Hillel, community center, *havurah* or Jewish college can help.

[26]The symbolism in Jewish foods plays a large role in our Rosh Hodesh gatherings. Recipe sources are in Siegel et al., 1973 and *The Spice and Spirit of Kosher Jewish Cooking* (NY: Bloch, 1977).

[27]*Mikveh* or purification is understood by the women who celebrate Rosh Hodesh to have a potentially positive connotation. We use water, when available, to enact our own informal *mikveh*. Alternatively, we also use song and movement and meditation as purifying agents. We take the concept of *mikveh*, lit. a gathering of waters, to mean a spiritual cleansing tool. For further reading on mikveh, see Adler, Rachel and Koltun; also Aryeh Kaplan, *Waters of Eden* (NY: Natl Conf. of Synagogue Youth, 1976).

[28]See Kaplan, pp. 49-50.

[29]Tractate *Sanhedrin* (41b-42a) says that as long as the moon is still waxing, up until the fifteenth day of the month the blessing for the new moon may be cited. From this we derive the authority to celebrate *Rosh Hodesh* when convenient for most group members anytime through mid-month.

[30]The letter was composed and used by Aviva Cohen-Kiener, 1984.

NOTES—TISHRE

[1] See Kitov for more on the holidays of *Tishre:* also Waskow, and Schauss, *The Jewish Festivals.*

Rosh Hodesh Tishre is the same as Rosh HaShanah and is not celebrated as a separate holiday. The new moon of *Tishre* is the time when the Jewish community "dips into the waters of the well" to drink together, a means of bringing the Messianic age closer.

Rosh Hodesh groups on whose experiences this book is based have never marked the new moon with both men and women. What we present here is our ideal for a Rosh Hodesh celebration. Until now this has been a hope and dream of the women who regularly observe the new moon together. Such a joint Rosh Hodesh would be the culmination of regular meetings of men or women only who have been exploring their unique relationships to God and to each other. Thus *Rosh Hodesh Tishre* would become a yearly reunion of men and women focusing on the insights gained in the separate groups the previous year. Of course, men and women would continue to mark the other Jewish holidays together as before.

See Pamela Faith Lerman and Arthur Waskow, "Beyond the Shabbos Bride," *Menorah*, January/February, 1984, Vol. 4, Nos. 11-12, for more on men and women creating liturgy together.

[2] *Mishnah Ta'anit* 4:8 in Epstein . See also the chapter on *Av* for more on the holiday of *Tu B'Av.*

[3] *Cohen-Kiener* paper on Judaism and astrology. See also: Astronomy, Astrology, Astrolabe, Rosh Hodesh, in *Encyclopaedia Judaica;* also specific months. See also Alan Oken's trilogy, *As Above, So Below, The Horoscope, The Road and Its Travellers,* and *Astrology: Evolution and Revolution* (NY: Bantam).

Resources in Hebrew: Solomon Ibm Gabirol's *Keter Malkhut* on the planets; *Sefer Yetsirah,* a brief cosmogony that includes astrological information; *B'raitah d'Mazalot,* a medieval midrash on astronomy, astrology and intercalation. Abraham Ibn Ezra, an important medievalist, wrote *Reshit Hokhmah,* on astronomy and astrology in his collected works.

⁴ *"Unetanah tokef"* prayer from Musaf of the Rosh HaShanah service in Rabbi Jules Harlow, ed. *Mahzor for Rosh HaShanah and Yom Kippur* (NY: 1972), p. 240.

⁵ Matt, pp. 33-39, and *Encyclopaedia Judaica,* Vol. 14: 1353-1354.

⁶ Adapted from Ginzberg, Vol. I:24. On the connection between the moon and women with its implications for Jewish women, see Arthur I. Waskow, "Feminist Judaism: Restoration of the Moon" in Heschel, pp. 261-272.

⁷ Personal tale collected from Pnina Peli, Jerusalem, April 14, 1980.

⁸ *Ibid.*

⁹ Cat Stevens on records "Tea for the Tillerman" and "Greatest Hits."

¹⁰Drorah Setel, original blessing. For more on creating alternatives to traditional blessings, see Marcia Falk, "What About God?", *Moment,* March, 1985, pp. 33-36.

¹¹Genesis 1:16.

¹²Sheila Peltz Weinberg, original blessing.

¹³Adapted from Ginzberg, Vol. I:65-66. For Jewish women's relationship through history to Lilith, see Aviva Cantor, "The Lilith Question," LILITH Magazine, Vol. 1, No. 1, 1976), and Barbara Black Koltuv, *The Book of Lilith,* forthcoming 1986, (NY: Samuel Weiser Co.)

¹⁴These insights on women's "voice" were expressed by Carol Rose, Correspondence, September, 1984.

¹⁵For an explanation of guided imagery and meditation, see Preface. This guided fantasy was based on ideas of Carol Rose of Winnipeg and Colette Aboulker-Muscat of Jerusalem.

¹⁶*Encyclopaedia Judaica,* Vol. 14:310.

¹⁷Music by Rabbi Shlomo Carlebach; words by Rafi Katz.

¹⁸Music by Pete Seeger, words from Ecclesiastes 3:1-8 in Milton Okun, ed. *Great Songs of the Sixties* (Quadrangle, 1970).

NOTES—HESHVAN

¹ Kitov, Vol. 1: 249-267.

² See Neumann and Hamilton, pp. 92-100.

³ See Part I, p. .

⁴ Dream of P.V. Adelman, Jerusalem, 1979.

⁵ This story was told each year at Rosh Hodesh as a way for women to explain the inherent difficulties and contradictions in being a Jewish woman. Rabbi Nachman tells of a king's son who thought he was a rooster. The king was desperate to have a normal heir to the throne and called in a wise man to cure his son. The wise man did so by allowing the rooster-prince to feel like a rooster inside while looking just like a human being on the outside.

This is an apt metaphor for the woman who does not feel like a full human being in the context of Judaism; further, she cannot feel like a full Jew in the context of secular society. The story can be found in Elie Wiesel, *Souls on Fire* (NY: 1972), pp. 170-171.

⁶ See Cohen.

⁷ Original midrash by P.V. Adelman based on Exodus 32:1-6 and Ginzberg, Vol. 3:121-122 also discussions of sources at Rosh Hodesh gatherings. This first appeared in slightly different form in *Reconstructionist,* June, 1985, pp. 16-18.

⁸ For classical Jewish sources cited on Jewish women being "reborn" each month like the moon, see Waskow essay in Heschel, pp. 261-272.

⁹ "Bereshit Rabba," Parshat VaYishlach, 82 in *Midrash Rabba.*

¹⁰For more on the universal existence of the menstrual taboo, see Douglas, Harding, and Shuttle and Redgrove.

¹¹See *Tishre,* Note 18.

¹²Arapaho Chant, Friction in the System, Eastbay Peoples Music, 2130 A Roosevelt Ave., Berkeley CA 94703; also in *Winds of the People,* p. 107.

¹³Joni Mitchell on her record, "Ladies of the Canyon" and in *Winds of the People,* p. 11.

¹⁴Words and music by Joni Mitchell on the album "Circle Game" by Tom Rush.

NOTES—KISLEV

¹ HaCohen, Vol. 6:275.

² For other writings on Jewish women lost or neglected in history, see *Response,* 1973, pp. 23-46; Koltun, pp. 139-178; Cantor bibliography; Elwell and Levenson; Sasso and Elwell; Taitz and Henry, *Written Out of History: Our Jewish Foremothers,* (Biblio Press, NY, 2nd ed. rev.) See also Judy Chicago, *The Dinner Party,* pp. 65 and 118.

³ Hebrew is made up of words consisting mostly of three-letter roots.

⁴ *Apocrypha,* "Book of Judith."

⁵ *Ibid.,* 11:12.

⁶ Poem by Carol Rose first read at Rosh Hodesh Kislev, Jerusalem, 1979.

⁷ *Apocrypha,* "Book of Judith," 15:12.

⁸ *Ibid.,* 16.

⁹ Tune by Maia Brumberg first sung at Rosh Hodesh Kislev, Jerusalem, 1979; words from "Book of Judith," 16:7-8; in *Menorah,* forthcoming.

¹⁰Ginzberg, Vol. 1:297.

¹¹Psalm 22:1.

[12]See *Exodus Rabbah* 15:6 for a comparison of Esther to the moon.

[13]Judges 4:4; Deborah is named one of seven prophetesses. (The others are: Sarah, Miriam, Hannah, Abigail, Hulda and Esther, in *Tractate Megilla* 14a)

[14]Original midrash by Janet Zimmern-Kahan first told at Rosh Hodesh Kislev, Boston, 1983. Deborah is referred to as a "woman of flames" in *Tractate Megillah* 14a in the Talmud.

[15]Tune by Suri Levow Krieger, first sung at Rosh Hodesh Kislev, Jerusalem, 1979; words from the liturgy for Hanukkah. This song may be found on the cassette *Hodesh Hodesh BaShir: A Song A Month,* available with this book from Biblio Press.

[16]Words by S. Levy-Tannai, music by I. Amiran.

[17]HaCohen, Vol. 6:275.

NOTES—TEVET

[1] Kitov, Vol.1:325-327; II Kings 25 and Jeremiah 52.

[2] Lamm, pp.202-203.

[3] Schauss, p.299. Suggested for study are these Torah portions about death: Moses' death in Deuteronomy 31:14-34 and Sarah's death in Genesis 23:1-20.

[4] *Encyclopaedia Judaica* 8:1461; Waldemar Janzen, *Mourning Cry and Woe Oracle* (NY:1972), p.16; Rosenblatt, Walsh and Jackson, *Grief and Mourning in Cross-Cultural Perspective* (New Haven:1976); Y. Sabar, "Lel-Huza: Story and History in a Cycle of Lamentations," *Journal of Semitic Studies,* Vol. 21:1 and 2, 1976.

[5] Book of Jeremiah, 9:16-17.

[6] For a tale of a goat appropriate this month, see "Rabbi Menachem Mendl of Kotsk and the Goat," in Wiesel, pp.251-252.

[7] The idea for a "memory jar" is from Erlbaum ms., p. 6.
Take a box or jar, one that belonged to or was given to you by the person whom you wish to remember. Fill it with your written thoughts and memories of the person. Write down anecdotal experiences or favorite expressions and place them in the container. Decorate it. Put pictures and special objects inside it.
If you fill the container with tangible things, you can always open it and experience these things again and again.
What requires more dedicated energy is to fill the box or jar with meditations—ideas you have written down—and then to tie a ribbon around it or seal it and hold onto it. You need never open the container again. The simple act of holding it, looking at it, and meditating with it transforms the container into an ark for your memories of the person.

[8] If it is difficult to remember specific stories about the deceased person, see Zeitlin, et al.

9 P.V. Adelman's memory of her paternal grandmother, Bella Jenkins Williams who passed away before Pesach, 1981.

10For Group Wailing in another context, see chapter on Tammuz.

11Hasidic melody from Zeller cassette tape.

12Tune by Rabbi Shlomo Carlebach; words by Rafi Katz.

13II Samuel 18:18.

14Tractate *Pirkei Avot* 4:17

15Personal tale of P.V. Adelman.

16This meditation is based on ideas from Matia Angelou and Lili Goodman.

17For other interpretations/explanations of Kaddish, see Schauss, pp.294-295 and Lamm, pp.147-187. See Weidman-Schneider, pp.143-148, for controversy over Jewish women saying Kaddish. An excellent description of one woman's attempt to say Kaddish for her mother is by Sara Reguer, "Kaddish from the 'Wrong Side of the Mehitzah," in Heschel, pp.177-181. The basis for women's exemption from saying Kaddish is discussed by Biale, pp.10-43. For the prayer itself, see Birnbaum, pp.49-52.

NOTES—SHVAT

1 For more information on the revival of the custom of the *Tu B'Shvat* Seder, send for "Seder for Tu B'Shvat," Bureau of Jewish Education, 333 Nahanton, Newton, MA or contact your local bureau. *A Tu B'Shvat Seder,* compiled by Rabbi Julie Gordon, is a guide for the celebration of *Tu B'Shvat* from a feminist perspective, from Jewish Women's Resource Center, NY.

2 Proverbs 3:18.

3 For a variation on this meditation see Starhawk, p.44.

4 This nickname was coined at one Rosh Hodesh in Jerusalem, 1979. "Nosh" is Yiddish for a snack. "Drash" is the process of making midrash, commentaries and stories based on the Torah. "Nosh 'n Drash" refers to a process of "feeding" with nourishing words and real food at the same time which occurs in the course of each Rosh Hodesh celebration.

"Drash" can be compared to playing in a jazz band where there is a base line from which each musician improvises, spinning out new melodies and then returning to the base line again. In our case, the particular verse from the Torah which is being studied is the "base line." Those who study together are the "musicians."

5 Original midrash by P.V. Adelman based on reference to "alon bachut" in Genesis 35:8.

6 Translation provided by Rabbi Susan Talve, St. Louis, Missouri.

[7] Seven prophetesses are referred to in Tractate *Megillah* 14a. See chapter on *Kislev,* Note 13.

[8] For an original midrash on Tamar as tree by P.V. Adelman, see *Reconstructionist,* January/February, 1986.

[9] See chapter on *Heshvan,* Note 6.

[10]To make the Almond Moon Dream Cake, add 1/4 cup of almond liquer to your favorite white cake recipe. Decorate with blanched and whole almonds.
For suggestions of ways to shape hallot, see Siegel et al, 1973, pp.38-39; also *Spice and Spirit* cookbook.

[11]The planting ritual is based on a gathering which took place in Shvat, 1981 in Philadelphia.

[12]Kitov, *The Book of Our Heritage,* Vol.1:347.

[13]Tune by Suri Levow Krieger and P.V. Adelman; words from Psalms 1:3; recorded on "A Song A Month" available from Biblio Press.

[14]For more on this story see *Encyclopaedia Judaica,* Vol.8.:964 and Vol.7:1154. It is also in Tractate *Ta'anit,* 19a, 23a.

[15]Words and music by Dave Mallet on the album *Dave Mallet;* also in *Winds,* p.29.

ADDENDA—ADAR ALEPH*

*Sample Torah Texts for Discussion**
a) Rabbi Akiba used to say: "Beloved (of God) is humankind for it was created in the image of God, but greater still was the love (shown to human beings) in that it was made known to them that they were created in the image of God," *(Pirkei Avot,* Sayings of the Fathers, 3:18).
These questions might be considered: what is the meaning of "image of God" and do you agree with Rabbi Akiba's statement?
b) It is said that the entire time the child is in the womb, it is being taught the Torah continuously by a special angel. When the child is about to emerge from the womb, the angel taps it under the nose and it forgets all that had been learned. This is why we are born with an indentation under our noses and also why we must spend our lives learning Torah. (Tractate *Niddah* 30)
Questions to consider are: what does this story mean? and what kind of power does this imply in the womb of the woman?
c) "R. Johanan said: Three keys the Holy One blessed but He has retained in His own hands and not entrusted to the hand of any messenger, namely, the Key of Rain, the Key of Childbirth, and the Key of the Revival of the Dead. The Key of Rain, for it is written, 'The Lord will open unto thee His good treasure, the heaven to give the rain of thy land in its season.' (Deuteronomy 28:12) The Key of Childbirth, for it is written, 'And God remem-

*Texts researched by Rabbi Cynthia Kravetz of Philadelphia.

bered Rachel and God hearkened to her and opened her womb.'" (Genesis 30:22) (Tractate
Ta'anit) 2)

Why and how are the keys of rain, childbirth, and the revival of the dead linked?

d) Another exposition: "If a woman produce offspring, etc." This is alluded to in what
is written, 'Who shut up the sea with doors, when it broke forth, and issued out of the womb
(Job 38:8) R. Eliezer and R. Joshua and R. Akiba gave explanations. R. Eliezer said: 'Just
as a house has doors, so a woman, too, has doors, as it is written, 'Because it shut not up the
doors of my (mother's) womb (Job 3:10).' R. Joshua said: 'Just as for a house there are keys
(mafteach), so, likewise, for a woman, as it is written, 'And God hearkened to her, and
opened *(patach)* her womb (Genesis 30:22).' R. Akiba said: 'Just as a house has hinges *(tzirim),*
as it is written, 'She knelt and gave birth, for her pangs *(tzirim)* came suddenly upon her (I
Samuel 4:19).' 'When it broke forth, and issued out of the womb,' by raising itself to issue
forth." *(Leviticus Rabbah,* Tazria, 14:4)

Reflect on the connections between the sea and the womb made above, especially in
reference to the Exodus story.

e) Whoever has children in the cradle had best be at peace with the world. (Yiddish
proverb)

How would you interpret this proverb and do you agree with its sentiment? Why/why
not?

NOTES—ADAR ALEPH (1)

[1] Rachel is known as the Compassionate Mother in Judaism. Her name means "ewe,"
a female sheep. Women pray to her especially concerning matters of childbirth, for she is
thought to intervene on behalf of the children of Israel. See Ginzberg, Vol.2:135-136.

[2] *Encyclopaedia Judaica,* "Rachael's Tomb," Vol.13:1489-1490. Regarding a contemporary prayer for fertility addressed to a compassionate female spirit, see P.V. Adelman, "A
Prayer for Fertility," *Reconstructionist,* June 1985, pp.26-27.

Another meaning of Rachel's compassion is portrayed in the chapter on *Tammuz.*

[3] Trachtenberg, p.48, pp.168-172.

[4] An excellent account of a pre-birth ritual is given in Shoshana Zonderman's "spiR-
ITUAL PREPARATION FOR PARENTHOOD," *Response:* The Family issue, pp.29-39.

[5] The entire ceremony for this Rosh Hodesh is based on the actual *Yoledet* of Tiferet
Sassona, daughter of Janet and Joseph Zimmern-Kahan which took place in Boston, Spring,
1983.

More accounts of birth rituals of Jewish girls are given by Broner, pp.1-8, 20-31;
Leifer and Leifer, in Koltun; "The Covenant of Washing," *Menorah,* April/May, 1983, Vol. 4,
Nos. 3-4. See articles and books on naming baby girls in Judaism, *Birth Ceremonies Guide* from
Jewish Women's Resource Center, NY; Sandy Eisenberg Sasso, *Call Them Builders,* (NY:
Reconstructionist Press, 1977); Weissler unpublished ms.; Margolis and Margolis, in Strass-
feld et al, 1976, p. 11-45; Weidman Schneider, pp.120-130.

Concerning adoption considered for birth rituals, see Strassfeld and Green, pp.20-22,
and Dan Shevitz, "A Guide for the Jewish Adoptive Parent," *Response* "Family" issue,
pp.107-126.

[6] For more on *sefirot,* see Scholem, pp.35-37; *Encyclopaedia Judaica,* Vol. 10:563-570;
and Matt, pp.216, 221, 222, 229.

[7] *Encyclopaedia Judaica,* Vol.5:43.

[8] Kitov, Vol.2:112.

[9] Rabbinic thesis of Rabbi Jeffrey A. Summit, "The Song of Songs in the Biblical tradition of the Yemenite Jews," ch.5. Hebrew Union College/Jewish Institute of Religion, Cincinnati: University Microfilms, 1979.

[10] Words and music by Alterman-Zaira in Theodore Bikel, *Folksongs and Footnotes* (NY: 1960), pp.104-105.

[11] Words by Sholom Aleichem, music by David Kovanovsky in Mlotek, pp.152-153.

[12] Also called *Shir Erev* (Evening song); words by M. Halpern; music by J. Engel.

[13] See the beginning of this chapter for a Pre-Birth/Pregnancy ritual.

[14] For a diagram of the *sefirot* which can be compared to the human body, see *Encyclopaedia Judaica,* Vol.10:635; see also Matt, pp.33-39.

[15] See chapter on *Sivan* for parallels between Ruth and Abraham.

[16] The meanings and numerical values of Hebrew letters have long been of interest to Jewish scholars. See *Encyclopaedia Judaica,* Vol.7:369-374 and Trachtenberg, pp.78-113.

[17] Music by P.V. Adelman, words from Song of Songs, tape cassette by Adelman and Krieger, "A Song a Month."

[18] Meditation composed by Lili Goodman.

[19] Genesis 1:9.

[20] Words spoken at the *Yoledet* of Tiferet Sassona by Barbara Blaustein, friend of Janet Zimmern-Kahan, the new mother.

ADDENDA—ADAR BET (2)

[9] Some of the stories behind the masks created on Rosh Hodesh Adar in Boston, are given here:

1. Woman: (wearing a mask of a dark, primitive face with bright orange and black designs painted on it) I am Astarte, Goddess of Love and Sexuality, a very distant relative of Queen Esther. Actually not so distant. Our names are related.

The idea for my mask comes from a dream I had a few weeks ago, a dream of Astarte in which I felt the enormous strength and power of the goddess. I made the mask in order to *become* her, to see how that would feel.

(The creator of this mask was the poet, known as "E.J." of Boston.)

2. Woman: (wearing a green mask from which leaves and flowers are growing) I am Health.

This past year I have come to grips with dying because I had a dangerous tumor. But I've been treated successfully and now know that I'll live for a long time. My mask is also based on a dream.

At the end of my treatment, I dreamt that I was at a beach with my two daughters. The ocean and sky and shore provided me with a strong sense of beauty and the eternal. One of my daughters started to walk out into the ocean, "to drown," she said," because she couldn't bear any more beauty. I waded out to save her. She fought me, but finally, I was able to pull her back to shore.

This dream meant Life to me. Wearing this mask after such a long time of being on the edge of life, the edge of the ocean, I feel like I'm ready to dance again, to be alive, to celebrate.

(The creator of this mask was the writer, Elana Klugman, of Boston.)

*

3. Woman: (wearing a sweet face with perfectly curled blonde hair, blue eyes, cherry-red lips) Once I knew a woman from Iran who was very dark with thick brown hair and deep brown eyes. Her only dream, she told me, was to be beautiful. To her, being beautiful meant having blonde hair, blue eyes, fair skin, just like a Hollywood movie star.

I made my mask in honor of this Iranian woman because I wish she could have believed enough in the strength of her own beauty instead of envying beauty that was not hers.

(The creator of this mask was a workshop participant from Northampton, Massachusetts.)

*

[10]The following suggestions for skits and issues to discuss were offered at a workshop conducted by Mary Gendler at Harvard Divinity School, Adar, 1976 on Esther and Vashti and the notion of role reversal.

1) How have you felt left out or excluded as Vashti did from a particular aspect of Jewish life? Think of an example and how you dealt with it, how you would have liked to act if you could have.

2) How are the themes of Hiddenness and Revelation portrayed in the Purim story, in the history of the Jewish people, in the lives of Jewish women? Consider the Exile of the Shekhinah and the quasi-invisibility of Jewish women throughout history. (See Scholem, pp.59-153.)

3) What would it be like to reverse all the female and male parts in the Purim story? Try it.

NOTES—ADAR BETH (2)

[1] Book of Esther, *The Writings.*

[2] Lynn Gottlieb, "The Secret Jew" in Heschel, pp.273-277; also in *Conservative Judaism,* vol.30, no.3 (Spring 1976), pp.59-62.

[3] These ideas came from a discussion with Aviva Cohen-Kiener and Pnina Peli, Jerusalem, 1979.

[4] Ginzberg, Vol. 4:365-381; see also Gendler in Koltun, and Aviva Cantor, "The Real Story of Esther," *Off Our Backs,* March, 1972.

[5] Esther 8:16.

6 *Exodus Rabbah* 15:6

7 Esther 4:16.

8 For additional material on Adar, Esther, Purimshpiels, see R. Adler; B. Greenberg, and Plaskow, "The Jewish Feminist: Conflict in Identities," in Koltun.

9 Refer to Addenda on pages preceding these Notes.

10Refer to Addenda on pages preceding these Notes.

NISAN—ADDENDA

More Legends of Miriam

Miriam, the Midwife*

While in Egypt, Miriam and her mother, Yocheved worked as midwives. Midwives are the bearers of sacred knowledge, distinguishing daily between life and death in the opening of the womb. Both women took other names to distinguish their daily lives from their lives as midwives. They were called Shiphrah (Yocheved) and Puah (Miriam).

A midrash states that Shiphrah was so called because she "straightened out" *(m'shappereth)* the arms and legs and neck of the newborn. Her name also contains the root, *Peh-Resh-Yud* which means "to be fruitful." Since she did not obey Pharoah's dictum to let the male babies die, the Children of Israel were indeed fruitful *(sh'paru)* in her day.

Puah was so named because she used to "cry out" *(po'ah)* to the child. In this way she brought it forth from the womb. The medieval commentator, Rashi, says that she knew how to say gentle words to coax the child into the light of day. She would blow a charm into the mother's ear and the child would hear.

Miriam, the Prophetess**

Miriam's father, Amram, had divorced Yocheved because he felt that by refraining from his duties as a husband, he could prevent more births. Thus, Pharaoh's intent to destroy all Jewish male babies would be foiled.

But Miriam challenged him: "Pharaoh has decreed that all boy babies be killed, but you are making things worse by preventing all female births as well."

Amram could not refute this. He remarried Yocheved. Again, Miriam's midwifely traits helped keep the Jewish people alive. Miriam knew of the greatness of her brother, Moses, even before he was born. The story of his life, how he would be saved from drowning in the Nile, How he would lead the Children of Israel out of certain death by drowning in the Sea of Reeds— it is said all this was revealed to Miriam, the prophetess even while her brother was still in the womb.

*Ginzberg, Vol.2:251; Tractate *Sotah* 11b.
**Ginzberg, Vol.2:262-265.

NOTES—NISAN

[1] Words from Song of Songs 2:12, Hebrew folk song.

[2] Ginzberg, Vol.3:317.

[3] Matt, p.44, 206. The Midrash holds that even the spirits of those yet unborn were at Mt. Sinai.

[4] Exodus 15:20-21.

[5] Tractate *Sotah* 11b.

[6] Introduced by Esther Linder, *Rosh Hodesh Nisan,* Philadelphia, 1979.

[7] The reference is to a haggadah in the abstract, one that has not yet been written although it is currently in the process of being written by participants in *Rosh Hodesh* rituals. This poem, written by P.V. Adelman, was first read at *Rosh Hodesh Nisan,* Philadelphia, 1981 and might be included in such a haggadah.

[8] See *Song of Songs Rabbah* 1:2 for a comparison of Torah to water.

[9] Genesis 21:24-25.

[10] Genesis 21:19.

[11] Genesis 26:18-23.

[12] *Bereshit Rabbah* 54:5, 60:5.

[13] Ginzberg, Vol.2:262-265.

[14] *Ibid.*

[15] Exodus 15:20-21.

[16] Cohen, pp.179-190.

[17] Numbers 21:17-18.

[18] Vilnay, *Agadot Eretz-Yisrael,* pp.182-184.

[19] Kitov, Vol.2:157-162.

[20] See Addenda preceding Notes for additional stories of Miriam from various sources. For a cross-cultural perspective on midwives, see Lois Paul and Benjamin D. Paul, "The Maya Midwife as a Sacred Specialist: A Guatamalan Case," *American Ethnologist* 2:4(1975), 707-726; see also Brigitte Jordan, *Birth in Four Cultures* (Quebec: Eden Press Women's Publications, Inc., 1978) p.27.

[21] Words and music by Suri Levow Krieger, on Adelman and Krieger, "A Song A Month," available from Biblio Press.

[22] Exodus 15:21.

ADDENDA IYYAR

Refer to Notes 14-15-17-18-19

STORYTELLING (See also Note 14)

Imagine yourself in your grandmother's kitchen sharing a glass of tea. She is telling you about her life, how she feels about herself, how she spends her days. Does something trouble her?

The women describe the imagined interaction. Questions:

(1) Did your grandmother work? (2) Did she work for money or for personal gratification? (3) Was she fulfilled in her work, rewarded? (4) Was her work belittled? (5) Was she frustrated in her different roles? (6) Would she have chosen another life?

Imagine yourself as a little girl in your mother's kitchen having a glass of milk. She speaks about her life, hopes and expectations. Using the previous questions, apply them to your mother.

Some additional questions; If your grandmother could give you a gift (value, character, trait), what would it be? Why? If your mother could give you a gift, what would it be? Why? If you could give such a gift to them, what would it be? Why?

In discussing the behavior of mother/grandmother, consider the following. Did she assume the role she did because: it was expected of her? she was afraid to change? to please her parents? of habit? or lethargy? of personal ambition? of her own free will? of other reasons?

Consider each role for mother and grandmother: What was expected of her? What gave her pleasure? What did she do to give pleasure to others? What was she most proud of? What was her biggest disappointment?

How are you like your mother/grandmother? How are you different from them?

DEMETER AND PERSEPHONE (see also Note 15)

1) What are the spiritual/life paths of the mother and daughter figures in the stories of Demeter and Persephone and Naomi and Ruth?

2) How are the stories similar or different?

3) What does the Biblical story teach? The Greek myth?

4) What do the relationships between Ruth and Naomi, between Ruth and Boaz, between Ruth and God teach us?

5) Can these relationships serve as models for human relationships in general? Why or why not?

Suggestion for a ritual to precede an adult Bat Mitzvah: (see also notes 17, 18, 19)

Many Jewish women of mature age are becoming Bat Mitzvah today. Motivating them is a desire to learn Hebrew, read Torah, lead a prayer service and become a literate Jew.

Ways of becoming bat mitzvah are as diverse as the women who decide to do it. Interviews with women throughout the U.S. who became bat mitzvah in their twenties and later, show that the synagogue service can be as traditional or innovative as one chooses.[18]

Rosh Hodesh provides a unique opportunity for the women's community to help the adult bat mitzvah prepare for her upcoming ceremony. On the *Rosh Hodesh* preceding the service, the bat mitzvah can invite female relatives and friends to give her support, to offer ideas for her *d'var Torah*, the learned discourse on the Torah portion which she will read in the synagogue. She can even practice her speech before this receptive audience.

The Keeper of the month should ask the bat mitzvah what she needs from the community of women, and try to fulfill these requests. This process is the same for any life cycle ritual—menarche, birth, menopause, death—where the Keeper must consider carefully the wishes of the woman marking the event before creating a ritual.

Some suggestions for preparing the bat mitzvah follow: (1) Study together the bat mitzvah's Torah portion; (2) Eat sweet foods (cookies, cakes, breads) baked in the shapes of Hebrew letters, a custom which marks the beginning of a Jewish child's learning; (3) Tell stories of "How I Decided to Learn Torah" or "How I Was Kept From Learning Torah"; (4) Sing songs about learning Torah or songs which contain the word Torah; (5) Create a prayer which a friend or relative would say upon the bat mitzvah of an older woman; (6) Devise a dance—*Keitsad m'rakdim lifnei ha bat mitzvah?* (How does one dance before the bat mitzvah?)—in the tradition of the dance one does before the bride.[19]

NOTES—IYYAR

[1]A ritual which has been performed and recorded is Irene Fine, *Midlife* (San Diego: Woman's Institute for Continuing Jewish Education, 1983). It also makes suggestions for creating a ritual. However, the book steers clear of an adequate recognition of the physiological implications of menopause for women's self-concept. The ritual was not created specifically for women.

[2]Williams and Williams (aka P.V. Adelman), pp.60-61. See also Myerhoff.

[3]See Douglas.

[4]Doress *et al.*, "Women Growing Older," *Our Bodies, Ourselves*, 1985 ed., pp.435-472.

[5]Book of Ruth, *The Writings*.

[6]Kitov, Vol.2:356-374.

[7]Kitov, Vol.2:363-366.

[8]See "How to Start a Group."

[9]*Encyclopaedia Judaica,* Vol.12:1382-1389.

[10]Paula Gantz, "Our Golden Years—You Should Live So Long!" in *Lilith,* Number 10, Winter, 1982-1983, pp.6-9; Louis Lowy, *Social Policies and Programs on Aging* (Lexington, Mass.: Lexington Books, D.C. Heath and Company, 1980), pp.16-17, 176-177.

[11]David Feldman, "The *Mitzvah* of Marital Sex," pp.60-80 and "The Legitimacy of Sexual Pleasure," pp.81-105 in Feldman, *Marital Relations, Birth Control and Abortion in Jewish Law* (New York: Schocken, 1968).

[12]Claudia Camp, "The Wise Women of II Samuel: A Role Model for Women in Early Israel?" in *The Catholic Biblical Quarterly,* Vol.43, No.1, January, 1981, pp.14-29.

[13]The witch in "Hansel and Gretel," the evil queen in "Snow White," the fairy god-mother in "Cinderella" are various examples of "wise women." See Brothers Grimm, *The Complete Grimm's Fairy Tales* (New York: Pantheon Books, 1944). See Tales 15, 53, and 21 esp.

[14]See Addenda Iyyar preceding Notes for alternative storytelling suggestions and exercises by Marcia Spiegel in a workshop, "Patterns and Changes: Grandmothers, Mothers, Daughters," presented at the Conference on Alternatives in Jewish Education, August 27, 1980, Univ. of Calif. at Santa Barbara.

[15]See Addenda Iyyar preceding Notes for discussion questions adapted from Hamilton, pp.49-53.

[16]This meditation created by Carol Rose, August, 1984.

[17]See Strassfeld and Green, p. 106; also Addenda Iyyar following Notes.

[18]Typical Bat Mitzvah ceremonies for older women were collected from Edith Benjamin of Canton, O. and Loni Pecker of Marlboro, Ma. For a Bar/Bat Mitzvah course for adults, contact Rabbi Gunter Hirschberg, Cong. Rodeph Sholom, 7 W. 83rd St., NY 10024.

[19]Bridal dance source: a Talmudic dispute as to "how does one dance before the bride?" See *Encylopedia Judaica,* Vol.II:1033 and the Talmudic tractate, *ketubbot* 16B-17A.

NOTES—SIVAN

[1]For suggestions regarding the celebration of puberty and coming of age for girls in Judaism, see Weidman-Schneider, pp. 130-142. This includes adult bat mitzvah as well. See the excellent workbook by Sasso and Elwell to stimulate discussion of the meaning of Jewish womanhood and how to celebrate bat mitzvah. For a history of Jewish women geared to younger readers, see Waxman *et al.*

Articles which outline the problems and issues involved in current bat mitzvah/puberty rites for Jewish girls are Corne, "The Bat Mitzvah Problem" in *Response,* Summer 1973, No.18, pp.114-116, and Koller-Fox, "Women and Jewish Education: A New Look at Bat Mitzvah," in Koltun, pp.31-42.

[2]Eliade, pp.41-60; Harding, pp.84-85.

[3]Book of Ruth, *The Writings* in JPS' *The Torah.*

[4]For further background material on the month of *Sivan,* the holiday of *Shavuot,* and the counting of the *omer,* see Kitov, Vol.3:50-159.

[5]Book of Ruth 3:11-13.

[6]Ginzberg, Vol.3:85-86; see story, "The Origins of *Rosh Hodesh"* in *Heshvan,* p. 26.

[7]Proverbs 1:8, 6:20.

[8]J. Gikatilla, *Sha'are Orah* (Gates of Light), quoted in Patai, p. 143.

[9]The concept of *hesed* in regards to Ruth's behavior is dealt with at length in Edward F. Campbell, Jr., transl., *Ruth/The Anchor Bible* (Garden City, N.Y.: Doubleday & Company, Inc., 1975), pp.29-31, 66, 81.

[10]Shuttle and Redgrove, pp.60-70; Harding, pp.84-85; H. Kamsler, "Hebrew Menstrual Taboos" in *Journal of American Folklore,* 51, pp.76-82.

[11]See chapter on Heshvan.

[12]Theodor Reik, *Pagan Rites in Judaism* (New York: Farrar, Strauss and Company, 1964), p.6.

[13]See Preface and chapters on *Tishre, Heshvan* for stories and materials on the origins of *Rosh Hodesh.* This is an appropriate time to restate the purpose and history of the group.

[14]See Adler, R. in Koltun where the Jewish blood taboo is explained in terms of the cycle of life and death.

[15]In the time set aside for Torah study, the *bogeret* may choose to study one Jewish woman or several women of history. See Note 2, *Kislev.*

[16]*Bereshit Rabbah,* "Hayyei Sarah," 81.

[17]*Ibid.*

[18]Original midrash by P.V. Adelman, 1982; with help from Judith Black, storyteller from Boston.

[19]Genesis 25:1-2.

[20]"Gifts" of smells were offered at a *Rosh Hodesh* gathering in Philadelphia, Spring, 1981.

[21]Sabbath liturgy for *Musaf* service, *"Eyn K'Eloheynu"* in Birnbaum, p.455.

[22]Menstrual blessings created by a women's ritual and prayer group called *Bat Kol* in the 1970's.

[23]The mother's speech was composed by Judy Petsonk and Susannah Heschel in an unpublished puberty ritual.

[24]See Siegel *et al.,* 1973, chapter on "Tallit."

[25]See Part I for further explanation of this midrash.

[26]These blessings are stated in Birnbaum, pp.5-6.

[27]See Note 24 above.

[28]Music and words by P.V. Adelman in *Menorah,* January-February, 1983, Vol.3, No.11-12, and in Strassfeld, Siegel, Elwell, and Setel, *The Jewish Calendar 5746* (New York: Universe), 1985, "week of January 19th."

[29]Words and music by Joni Mitchell.

[30]Words by M. Dor, music by Josef Hadar in Pasternak, p.11. The seven species are listed in Deuteronomy 8:8.

ADDENDA—TAMMUZ

Creating a Ritual for Divorce:

A ritual for divorce might include elements of both mourning and strength, signalling the status of an independent woman. The one undergoing divorce should decide when she needs to make a formal emotional and spiritual end of her marriage in her community of women. Legal proceedings effect this closure in the law courts, whether civil or religious, but fail to address the inner turmoil of the divorcée. Here are some suggestions for elements to be included in a ritual of divorce:

1) Cast away, destroy or burn a physical object which symbolizes the marriage, as in burning *Mitzrayim* (see *Nisan,* p. 60) or *Tashlikh* (see *Tishre,* p. 19).

2) Allow time to mourn for the marriage, for the loss of a relationship and a spouse, as well as time to experience hope for future growth and relationships.

3) Determine what is to be done with the old name. Will it be retained or released? How will this be decided?

4) Reflect on the meaning of being alone versus being a couple.

5) What will one's attitude be towards men, towards married friends? What will be sought in the next relationship?

6) Refer to Jewish tradition on the subject of divorce and learn what may be positive or negative there.[26]

Like other landmarks in the life cycle, divorce signals change in a woman's status and lifestyle. It may be seen as an initiation into a mature stage of single womanhood.[27]

NOTES—TAMMUZ

[1]Variants of this myth are found among peoples of the ancient Near East as well as the Greeks and Romans. Tammuz is also known as Attis, Adonis, Dammuzi, Osiris and Persephone. Innini is known as Cybele, Venus, Ishtar, Isis and Demeter.

The myth has several possible origins. One may stem from the practice of child sacrifice during a time of distress or disaster when a ruler might offer up his child to the gods as a means of appeasement. Or the myth of Tammuz may originate from the cycle of nature, as crops die during midsummer and resume in the rainy season, so does Tammuz descend to the underworld, re-emerging later as a living being.

The myth of Tammuz may be found in Langdon, Vol. 7:336-351. See also Diane Wolkstein and Samuel Kramer, *Inanna* (NY: Harper & Row, 1983).

[2]Book of Samuel, I and II, *Prophets* of the JPS *Torah, Prophets, and Writings.*

[3]Ezekiel 8:14.

[4]Genesis 8:9.

[5]Exodus 32:19.

[6]Kitov, Vol.3:193-203.

[7]See suggestions for a ritual of divorce in Addenda of this month.

[8]See Music Sources, Zeller cassette.

[9]*Pesikta Rabbati,* Piska 43, pp.752-768.

[10]I Samuel 1:13.

[11]Midrash/Ballad of Hannah by P.V. Adelman, 1983.

[12]Emily Dickinson in *The Complete Poems of Emily Dickinson.* Thomas H. Johnson, ed., (Boston: Little, Brown & Company, 1960), p.254.

[13]*Ibid.*

[14]Story collected from Maia Brumberg at a Rosh Hodesh celebration in Boston, 1981.

[15]Biale, pp.147-174, about the laws of *Niddah.*

[16]See the *Adar Aleph* for a different use of the cord from Rachel's Tomb.

[17]For more on the custom of adding a stone to a gravesite during a visit to honor the dead, see *Encyclopaedia Judaica,* "Holy Places," Vol.8:922.

[18]See the midrash on the twin sisters in Part I, p. 8.

[19]The story of Hannah is read each year as the *Haftarah* for the first day of *Rosh HaShanah.*

[20]Erlbaum, pp.11-12.

[21]For a *techina,* a Jewish woman's prayer in Yiddish, to the four matriarchs, see Siegel and Rheins, eds., *The Jewish Almanac* (New York: Bantam, 1980); for the original version in Yiddish see *Siddur Bait Yisrael,* Hebrew Publishing Co. A modern prayer on this same subject was written by Rabbi Rebecca Alpert, "A Prayer on the Occasion of a Miscarriage or Abortion," *Reconstructionist,* 51/1 (September 1985), p.4.

[22]See Notes for *Tevet,* no.4.

[23]See Part II, *Tevet,* for Group Wailing in another context.

[24]Folk song on the album by Priscilla Herdman, *The Water Lily.*

[25]I am indebted to my editor, Doris Gold, and my teacher, Phyllis Gorfain, folklorist from Ohio, for their wise words concerning a ritual of divorce. (See Addenda Tammuz preceding these Notes.)

[26]See Biale, pp.70-101, for a summary of Jewish divorce law; Weidman Schneider, pp.355-370, for resources on divorce for Jewish women in the U.S.A. and Israel; contact Pnina Peli active in reforming divorce law in Israel through Family League for Rights in the Courts, P.O.B.506, Netanya, Israel 42105; for the personal struggle of a Jewish single mother, see Sheila Peltz Weinberg, "the Jewish Single-Parent Family" in *Response: The Family,* Spring, 1985, No.48, pp.77-84; several women's prayers concerning divorce and its aftermath are included in Mitchell Salem Fisher, *Rebel, O Jews! and Other Prayers* (New York: Reconstructionist Press, 1973).

[27]To understand how a divorce may be seen as an initiation rite into another stage of life, see Eliade, pp.1-20.

NOTES—ELUL

[1]See Addenda following these notes.

[2]Kitov, Vol.3:319-332.

[3]See Gilligan, "Concepts of Self and Morality," pp.64-105.

[4]See Note 12 below.

[5]*Kavannot* were collected during a pre-wedding ritual for Esther Linder in Jerusalem, 1980.

[6]For alternative readings on the subject of love in its many forms, see the works of the Greek poet, Sappho (ca.600 B.C.E.); the Greek myths of Amor and Psyche, Atalanta and Hippomens, Endymion and Artemis, the works of Emily Dickinson, Adrienne Rich, Marge Piercy, and Torton Beck.

[7]I.L. Peretz, "The Match," in Esther Hautzig, transl. *The Case Against the Wind.* New York: Macmillan Publishing Co., Inc., 1975, pp.45-54.

[8]Sarah Bas-Tuvim was the 17th century author of a booklet of prayers, *"Shlyshe Sheorim,"* (Three Gates) written in Yiddish for women. See *Encyclopaedia Judaica,* Vol.4:318.

[9]An example follows this chapter. See Addenda.

[10]The bride's walk of seven sacred circles around the groom is a traditional one. Today, some couples have changed it into a walk around each other. For an explanation of this and

other marriage customs, see Goodman and Goodman, and Diamant; also Siegel et al., 1973, pp.158-166.

[11]The story of "The Singing Bride" and the meditation following it were collected from Carol Rose, 1982. See p. 113 for preparing to meditate.

[12]For an explanation of *mikveh* (purification through water), see Adler, Rachel and Siegel, *et al,* 1973, pp.167-171.

[13]Used with permission of M. Ackelsberg, D. Hirsch and D. Setel.

[14]Jewish folk belief.

[15]Carol Rose wrote this for the wedding of Zalman and Elana Schacter-Shalomi of Philadelphia.

[16]Song of Songs, 4:1-11.

[17]Original tune by P.V. Adelman; words from Song of Songs 5:1; on Krieger and Adelman, "A Song A Month" cassette tape.

[18]Scottish; on Judy Collins, *Maid of Constant Sorrow.*

[19]English traditional; in *Sing Together Children,* available from World Around Songs, Ret. 5, Burnsville, N.C. 28714.

[20]Instructions for blowing a *shofar* were provided by Suri Levow Krieger.

ADDENDA—ELUL*

[1]The ritual we present marks a union occurring at the more traditional end of the relationship spectrum—the marriage of a Jewish woman to a Jewish man. However, today partners of the opposite sex are celebrating unions, not necessarily marriages, sanctioned by community custom without the blessing of a rabbi or Jewish law. Partners of the same sex are sanctifying a lifelong commitment to each other before a community which will accept such a bond, without the presence of a rabbi representing Jewish law. Partners where one is Jewish and the other is not, are "wedding" their lives together, whether or not the Jewish establishment calls their ceremony a Jewish wedding.

The Jewish community must wrestle with the question: What constitutes a Jewish marriage? Is it the promise of children, when many couples now choose to be childless or unable to produce offspring of their own? Is it the making of a Jewish home, a Jewish way of life? Is the utterance of certain traditional vows before a required number of witnesses necessary as the divorce rate escalates? What is the meaning of "commit-

*A "Ritual for *Rosh Hodesh Elul"* which focuses mainly on preparation for the New Year as opposed to preparation for a wedding has been composed by Ruth M. Fingerhut of the Twin Cities Women's Minyan. Requests for copies may be made to Ms. Fingerhut c/o Biblio Press.

ment?" What can modern Judaism teach us about it and what has historical Judaism omitted? These questions form the background for the pre-wedding ritual given. Each Jewish women's community must determine what is meaningful and appropriate as a pre-wedding ritual for their own purposes.

Many of the ideas in this chapter which challenge the traditional notions of the Jewish wedding have come from discussions with *B'not Esh.*

9A Personal Tale: The Bride's Story

I've been afraid to give up my freedom, my singleness. For years I was eager to give it away so I wouldn't have to think on my own.

Most of you here know, I went through a lot of relationships, a lot of throwing myself away so I wouldn't have to face myself. Now I'm much stronger. But I still have a hard time imagining it: spending the rest of my life with one man and actually saying I'll do it, committing myself to it in front of you, my friends and relatives.

A memory of the desert keeps coming back to me. When Shmuel and I went camping in the Sinai peninsula, in Nuweiba by the Red Sea, we saw palm trees enclosed in barbed wire fences. Such a strange sight. Here's this tall, slender date palm surrounded by acres and acres of white sand. Not a hut or a tent in sight. But this voracious-looking fence surrounding it.

Turns out the fence was protecting the tree from all kinds of animals excreting on it, chewing it, from tourists climbing it and attaching ropes to it for holding tarps. That way the Bedouin could count on two things crucial for survival: a plentiful date harvest every season and welcome shade.

I was angry when I saw the palm tree fenced in, the way I used to think of marriage. But now I feel differently—marriage is the fence that defines the boundaries for a man and a woman. It also protects and conserves the couple. The tree and the Bedouin have a contract—she produces fruit so *he* can live and he protects her from the destructive forces of people and nature, watering her when she's dry, picking her fruits when she's ripe. So *she* can live. Of course, marriage only starts with this contract. But the contract provides the root for the relationship.

A palm tree growing in the desert alone doesn't need the fence, but once she begins to live within the context of human society, she requires protection, boundaries.

(told by P.V. Adelman at her pre-wedding
celebration in Philadelphia, 1980)

ADDENDA—AV

Ritual of Tu B'Av/Fifteenth of Av: A Midsummer Dance

Invite those who enjoy dancing; singles and couples, male and female, young and old. It may be celebrated any time from the 15th of the month (full moon) until the end of the month. If possible, it should be held as close as possible to the actual 15th of Av.

Bring: musical instruments, food and drink. Wear simple white garments.

Setting: Late afternoon, outdoors, in a field or a flat cleared space. If indoors, decorate with summer fruits and flowers. Space chosen should be large enough for full attendance.

The occasion should have dancing, singing and riddling, which follow. (See History below)

Singing: Some bring guitars, drums, bells and other instruments for accompaniment. Suggested love songs are: *Erev Shel Shoshanim*,[20] *K'Shoshanah Ben HaChochim*,[21] *Dodi Li*,[22] I Gave my Love a Cherry (Traditional), I Know Where I'm Going.[23]

Dancing: We use dances of American square dance and Israeli traditions, which should last into the night.[24] Food and drink should be on hand to sustain and inspire us. With luck and well-tuned *kavannah*, the old festival of Tu B'Av will reclaim its rightful place in the custom of matchmaking.

Riddling: In imitation of King Solomon and the Queen of Sheba, we have a riddle fest, a universal courting custom. The sexes alternate asking each other tricky riddles. The actual riddles of Solomon and Sheba may be used.[25] Include original ones as well.

History:

The 15th of Av is a minor holiday. Several events in Jewish history have contributed to the day's festive character.

On this day, God's decree of death for the desert generation was halted. Earlier it was said that because the Israelites had lost their faith when they sent spies into the Promised Land, believing the stories that Canaan was "a land which devours its inhabitants,"[26] they were doomed to lose many of the population as a punishment on the 9th of Av.

For forty years, the Israelites wandered in the desert, unable to enter their Promised Land. One year, Tisha B'Av came and went with no deaths. When the moon was full on the 15th, they knew that the death decree must have been lifted and so they rejoiced.

There is also an agricultural aspect of the date influencing this event, which falls on the full moon of midsummer, the time when the last wood of the season was cut and brought to the altar for kindling the eternal flame. Known as the "day of breaking the hatchets," it was marked during the time of the second Temple. Midsummer fire festivals are ancient and widespread in origin, usually representing a purging of evil influence before the fall harvest.[27] Tu B'Av was also the last day of the year for planting in Israel.

This date is even now considered appropriate for weddings.

> Thus did the Sages say: "No days were as festive to Israel as the Fifteenth of
> Av and Yom Kippur. On those days the daughters of Jerusalem used to go
> out dressed in white, and wearing garments that were loaned (so that all
> might be equal). A princess borrowed from a daughter of a Cohen Gadol;
> the daughter of the Cohen Gadol, from the daughter of his assistant
> cohen . . . And all Israel borrowed from one another, in order not to shame
> the poor.
> . . . And the daughters of Jerusalem went out and danced in the vineyards
> (outside the city). Whoever had no wife went there . . .[28]

Since the destruction of the Temple, the day was changed from one of revelry to a time for studying Torah. However, we have here decided to revive the ancient joyous festival. As single women, we reclaim the notion of being active in choosing a mate within a Jewish context. We take the sacred act of *shiddukhn*, making matches, into our own hands.[29] We claim the right to determine our own fate, which may also include choosing a partner of the same sex. All of the activities included above may be modified to suit the sexual preferences of those involved.

NOTES—AV

[1]Kitov, Vol. 3:308-309; Mishnah Ta'anit 4:8. See Addenda preceding these notes for ritual for Tu B'Av.

[2]Isaiah 29:1.

[3]Katia Molodowsky, "God of Mercy," in Spiegel and Lipton Kremsdorf, Eds.

[4]Suggestion for chant by Maia Brumberg, *Rosh Hodesh Av* in Boston, 1981; words from Lamentations 1:16.

[5]Words from Psalm 137; music by Salomone Rossi (1600).

[6]See *Tammuz,* Note 8.

[7]*Encyclopaedia Judaica* provides an introduction to Kabbalah, Vol. 10:621-624 on meanings and uses of Hebrew letters; Vol.10:617-619 for an explanation of the exile of the *Shekhinah.*

[8]Traditional Hasidic tale.

[9]The Havurah movement of the 1960's which continues into the present, is one example of a modern attempt to "rebuild" the Temple. See Siegel et al, 1973; Joel Rosenberg, "Havurat Shalom: An Appreciation at 10," *Genesis 2,* September/October 1978.

[10]The separate and distinct roles of activity for men and women in traditional orthodox Judaism are discussed at length in Part I.

[11]Words and music by Suri Levow Krieger, *A Song A Month* cassette tape.

[12]Words from Isaiah; music by Shlomo Zolty.

[13]Words and music by Abraham Goldfaden, from the 1880 operetta, Shulamis; in Mlotek, pp.4-6.

[14]Music and words by P.V. Adelman; see *Sivan,* Note 28.

[15]I am grateful to the ideas of Benji Jackson in preparing this meditation. See also Part I, p. 12-14.

[16]Vision of a *mishkan* collected from Carol Rose in an interview, Jerusalem, 1980.

[17]Words from the liturgy; music by Rabbi Shlomo Carlebach.

[18]Lawrence Kushner, *The Book of Letters* (NY: Harper and Row, 1975); Ben Shahn, *The Alphabet of Creation* (NY: Schocken, 1965); both serve as inspiration and insight for this exercise. See also Mark Podwal, *A Book of Hebrew Letters* (Philadelphia: Jewish Publication Society, 1978).

[19]Original tale by P.V. Adelman.

[20]Words by M. Dor, music by Josef Hadar in Pasternak, p. 11.

[21]Words from Song of Songs 2:2-3; music by Avshalom Katz in Pasternak, p. 12.

[22]Words from Song of Songs, traditional melody in Winds, p. 37.

[23]Scottish, *Ibid*, p. 38.

[24]Israeli folk dance instruction is found at a local Hillel, Jewish community center or synagogue.

[25]Ginzberg, Vol. IV: 145-149.

[26]Numbers 13:32.

[27]Kitov, Vol. 3:302-314; Schauss, p. 277. For a universal account of fire festivals see James Frazer, *The Golden Bough* (NY: Macmillan, 1922), pp.720-753. (Frazer received his information from accounts of travelers, a recognized flaw in his work)

[28]*Mishnah Ta-anit* 4:8.

[29]For a story on the difficulties of true matchmaking, see *Genesis Rabbah* 68:4 or its translation in Francine Klagsbrun, *Voices of Wisdom* (Philadelphia: Jewish Publication Society, 1980) pp.116-119.

BIBLIOGRAPHY

Adler, Margot. *Drawing Down the Moon*. NY: Viking, 1979.

Adler, Rachel. "The Jew Who Wasn't There," *Response*, Summer, 1973. 77-82.

——. "Tumah and Taharah: Ends and Beginnings," in Koltun, Elizabeth, Ed., *The Jewish Woman: New Perspectives*, NY: Shocken, 1976.

Agus, Arlene. "This Month Is For You," In Koltun.

Babylonian Talmud, Ed. I. Epstein. London: The Soncino Press, 1935.

Beck, Evelyn Torton. *Nice Jewish Girls: A Lesbian Anthology*, Watertown, Ma., Persephone Press, 1982. (Rept. Crossing Press, Trumansburg, NY, 1984)

"Bereshit Rabba," *Midrash Rabba*. Jerusalem: P'er Torah, 1969.

Biale, Rachel. *Women and Jewish Law*. NY: Shocken, 1984.

Birnbaum, Philip. Tr. *Daily Prayer Book: Ha-Siddur Ha-Shalem*. (Seph.) NY: Hebrew Publishing Co., 1969.

Book of Judith, *Apocrypha of the Old Testament*, Rev. NY: Thomas Nelson & Sons, 1957.

Boston Women's Health Book Collective. *Our Bodies, Ourselves*. NY: Simon & Schuster. (Editions of 1973 and 1985)

Broner, Esther M. *A Weave of Women*. NY: Bantam Books, 1978. Rept. Indiana University Press, 1985.

Cantor, Aviva. *The Jewish Woman: 1900-1980 Bibliography.* Fresh Meadows, NY: Biblio Press, 1982.*

_____. "The Lilith Question," *Lilith,* v. 1, no. 1, Fall, 1976.

Chicago, Judy. *The Dinner Party.* NY: Anchor/Doubleday, 1979.

Christ, Carol P. and Plaskow, Judith. *Womanspirit Rising: A Feminist Reader in Religion.* NY: Harper & Row, 1979.

Clark, Linda; Ronan, Marian and Walker, Eleanor. *Image Building.* NY: Pilgrim Press, 1981.

Cohen, Norman. "Miriam's Song: A Modern Midrashic Reading," *Judaism,* Spring, 1984.

Diamant, Anita. *My Beloved, My Friend.* NY: Summit Books, 1985.

Douglas, Mary. *Purity and Danger:* An Analysis of the Concepts of Pollution and Taboo. Boston: Routledge & Kegan, 1984.

Eliach, Yaffa. *Hasidic Tales of the Holocaust.* NY: Oxford Univ. Press, 1982.

Eliade, Mircea. Tr. Willard R. Trask, *Rites and Symbols of Initiation.* NY: Harper & Row, 1958.

Elwell, Sue Levi & Levenson, Edw. R. *Jewish Women's Studies Guide.* (1st ed.) Fresh Meadows, NY: Biblio Press, 1982.

Encyclopedia Judaica. Jerusalem: Keter Publishing House, 1972.

Erlbaum, Sheila Judith. "Separating and Saying Goodbye," Unpublished ms. Philadelphia, 1982.

Fiorenza, Elisabeth Schussler. *Bread Not Stone: The Challenge of Feminist Biblical Interpretation.* Boston: Beacon Press, 1985.

Geertz, Clifford. *The Interpretation of Cultures.* NY: Basic Books, 1973.

---

*out of print; new edition forthcoming.

Gendler, Everett, "Ten Feminine Archetypes in the Jewish Bible," *Response,* Summer, 1980.

Gilligan, Carol. *In A Different Voice.* Cambridge, Ma.: Harvard Univ. Press, 1982.

Goodman, Philip & Hannah. *The Jewish Marriage Anthology.* Philadelphia: Jewish Publication Soc. of America, 1971.

Govrin, Michal. "The Journey of the Year," First International Conf. & Festival of Jewish Theater. Tel Aviv, July, 1982. Unpublished ms.

Greenberg, Blu. *On Women and Judaism: A View From Tradition.* Philadelphia: Jewish Publication Soc. of America, 1981.

Ha-kohen, Israel Meir (Chafez Chaim). *Mishnah Berurah.* Tel Aviv: Merkaz L'Hinukh Torani, 1976.

Hamilton, Edith. *Mythology.* Boston: Little Brown & Co., 1940.

Harding, Esther M. *Woman's Mysteries.* NY: Bantam, 1971.

Heschel, Susannah. *On Being a Jewish Feminist: A Reader.* NY: Schocken, 1983.

Jewish Women's Resource Center, National Council of Jewish Women, Manhattan Chapter, 9 E. 69th St., NY 10021. Newsletters, esp. vol. II, Nos. 2 and 3, Winter/Spring, 1981, pertaining to *Rosh Hodesh.* (This center also provides guides to women's life cycle rituals)

Kaplan, Aryeh. *Jewish Meditation: A Practical Guide.* NY: Shocken, 1985.

Kitov, Eliyahu. *The Book of Our Heritage.* Vols I, II, III. NY: Feldheim, 1978.

Koltun, Elizabeth, Ed. *The Jewish Woman: New Perspectives.* NY: Shocken, 1976.

Lamm, Maurice. *The Jewish Way in Death and Mourning.* Middle Village, NY: Jonathan David, 1969.

Langdon, Stephen Herbert. "Semitic," in MacCulloch and Moore, Eds., Vol. 5, *The Mythology of All Races*. Boston: Marshall Jones Co., 1931.

Levow, Suri. *The Effect of Creative Ritual, Myth and Symbolism on Group Dynamics in the Rosh Hodesh Celebration*. (Doctoral Diss., Temple University, Philadelphia, 1981)

Matt, Daniel Chanan, Ed./Tr. *Zohar: The Book of Enlightenment*. NY: The Paulist Press, 1983.

Midrash Rabbah, Tr. H. Freedman and M. Simon. London: Soncino Press, 1939.

Myerhoff, Barbara, "Bobbes and Zeydes," in Judith Hoch-Smith and Anita Spring, Eds., *Women in Ritual and Symbolic Roles*. NY: Plenum Press, 1978.

Neumann, Erich. *Amor and Psyche: The Psychic Development of the Feminine*. Princeton, NJ: Princeton, Univ. Press, 1960.

Nietzche, Frederick. Tr. Walter Kauffman. *The Birth of Tragedy*. NY: Vintage Books, 1967.

Noy, Dov. *Motif-Index of Talmud-Midrashic Literature*. Ann Arbor, Mi.: University Microfilms, 1954. (Doctoral Dissertation series, pub. #8792)

Patai, Raphael. *The Hebrew Goddess*. NY: Avon Books, 1967.

Pesikta Rabbati: Discourses for Feasts, Fasts and Special Sabbaths. Ed. Leon Nemoy. New Haven: Yale University Press, 1968.

Pirkei Avot: Sayings of the Fathers. (See Babylonian Talmud)

Plaskow, Judith. "Language, God and Liturgy: A Feminist Perspective," *Response* #13, Spring, 1983, p.3-14.

Response issue on "The Family," Spring, 1985 and "The Jewish Woman, an Anthology," Summer, 1973.

Reuther, Rosemary Ruether, Ed. *Religion and Sexism*. NY: Simon & Schuster, 1974.

_____. *Womanguides: Readings Toward a Feminist Theology.* Boston: Beacon Press, 1985.

Sasso, Sandy Eisenberg and Elwell, Sue Levi. *Jewish Women: A Mini-course.* Denver: Alternatives in Religious Education, 1983.

Schauss, Hayyim. Tr. Samuel Jaffe. *The Jewish Festivals.* NY: Shocken, 1938.

_____. *The Lifetime of a Jew.* NY: Union of American Hebrew Congregations, 1978.

Schneider, Susan Weidman. *Jewish and Female: Choices and Changes in Our Lives Today.* NY: Simon & Schuster, 1984.

Scholem, Gershon. *On the Kabbalah and Its Symbolism.* NY: Shocken, 1969.

Schram, Penninah. "One Generation tells Another: The Transmission of Jewish Values Through Storytelling," *Literature in Performance,* April, 1984.

Shuttle, Penelope and Redgrove, Peter. *The Wise Wound: Eve's Curse and Everywoman.* NY: Richard Marek, 1978.

Siegel, Richard; Strassfeld, Michael; Strassfeld, Sharon, Eds. *The First Jewish Catalog.* Phila.: Jewish Publication Soc., 1973.

Spiegel, Marcia C. and Kremsdorf, Deborah Lipton. *Women Speak To God: The Prayers and Poems of Jewish Women.* San Diego: Woman's Inst. for Continuing Jewish Education. (Forthcoming 1986)

Starhawk. *The Spiral Dance.* NY: Harper & Row, 1979.

Strassfeld, Sharon and Strassfeld, Michael, Eds. *The Second Jewish Catalog.* Phila.: Jewish Publication Soc., 1976.

Strassfeld, Sharon and Green, Kathy. *The Jewish Family Book.* NY: Bantam Books, 1981.

Talve, Susan. *Birkat Halevanah: Blessing of the Moon.* (Rabbi's unpublished ritual guide) St. Louis, Mo., 1983.

The Torah, The Prophets, The Writers, 3 vols. Phila.: Jewish Publication Soc., 1962.

Trachtenberg, Joshua. *Jewish Magic and Superstition.* NY: Atheneum, 1975.

Vilnay, Ze'ev. *Agadat Eretz-Yisrael.* Jerusalem: Kiriat-Sefer, 1981.

Waskow, Arthur. *Seasons of Our Joy.* NY: Bantam Books, 1982.

Waxman, Meyer; Ish-Kishor, Sulamith; Sloan, Jacob. *Blessed Is The Daughter.* NY: Shengold, 1959.

Weissler, Chava. *New Jewish Birth Rituals for Baby Girls.* Unpublished ms. Dept. of Folklore/Folklife, Univ. of Pa.

Williams, Selma and Williams, Pamela (aka P.V. Adelman). *Riding the Nightmare: Women and Witchcraft.* NY: Atheneum, 1978.

Woolf, Virginia. *A Room of One's Own.* NY: Harcourt, Brace, Jovanovitch, 1963.

Woman's Institute for Continuing Jewish Education. *On Our Spiritual Journey:* A Creative Shabbat Service. San Diego, Ca.; 1984.

Zeitlin, Steven J., Kotkin, Amy J. and Baker, Holly Cutting. *A Celebration of American Family Folklore.* NY: Pantheon, 1982.

MUSIC SOURCES*

Adelman, Penina V. and Krieger, Suri Levow. "A Song A Month," cassette tape of original songs, voice and accompaniment, (prod. by Adelman & Levow) Available from Biblio Press, Fresh Meadows, NY 11365-0022.

Bikel, Theodore. *Folksongs and Footnotes.* NY: Meridian, 1960.

Coopersmith, Harry. *Choral Book of Jewish Songs.* NY: Bureau of Jewish Education, 1969.

Eisenstein, Judith Kaplan. *Heritage of Music,* NY: Union of American Hebrew Congregations, 1972.

Mlotek, Eleanor Gordon. *Mir Trogn a Gezang.* (Yiddish) NY: Workmen's Circle Education Dept., 1982.

Pasternak, Velvel. *Great Songs of Israel.* NY: Tara Publications/Board of Jewish Education, 1976.

Seasons of our Lives: Jewish Music for Life Cycle Occasions. 1986 Jewish Music Kit. JWB Jewish Music Council, 15 E. 26th St., New York 10010.

Winds of the People. Folksong lyrics booklet in English available from most folk music organizations.

Zeller, David. "Ruach: Chants and Songs," cassette tape, available from Zeller Productions, 620 Taylor Way, #14, Belmont, Ca. 94002.

---

*See Chapter Notes for specific music references suggested for monthly rituals.

143

MIRIAM'S WELL MUSIC

sung by Penina V. Adelman and Suri Levow Krieger

High Quality TDK Tape Cassette, 15 minutes each side

with instrumental accompaniment

A SONG A MONTH
(Hodesh Hodesh B'Shir)

Price: Postpaid, $6.00, with MIRIAM'S WELL.
or $9.00 ea. without book.

Available only from

BIBLIO PRESS, POB 22,
Fresh Meadows, NY 11365-002.

(Please prepay for 4th cl bookrate shipment)